Our Secret Territory

Our Secret Territory

THE ESSENCE OF STORYTELLING

LAURA SIMMS

First Sentient Publications edition 2011
Copyright © 2011 by Laura Simms

A paperback original

Cover and book design by Kim Johansen, *Black Dog Design* (www.blackdogdesign.com)
Cover art by Susan Leopold

Library of Congress Cataloging-in-Publication Data

Simms, Laura.
  Our secret territory : the essence of storytelling / Laura Simms.
    p. cm.
  Includes bibliographical references.
  ISBN 978-1-59181-172-5
  1. Storytelling. I. Title.
  LB1042.S55 2011
  808.5'43—dc22
                                2010041843

Printed in the United States of America

10 9 8 7 6 5 4 3 2 1

SENTIENT PUBLICATIONS
A Limited Liability Company
1113 Spruce Street
Boulder, CO 80302
www.sentientpublications.com

Let us now crawl under the canopy

of the currant leaves,

and tell stories.

Let us inhabit the underworld.

Let us take possession of our secret territory.

—Virginia Woolf, *The Waves*

To the memory of Carolyn Gould,
Albert Bouwmeester, Rachael Kessler, and
Vi Hilbert – you were the guides
who opened the way.

Contents

Foreword

$\mathcal{M}$ANY YEARS AGO, I was asked what medicine I carried. "Story is my medicine," I answered. For several years now, I have been gathering people around a fire to tell stories and bring healing to themselves, each other, the community, and the planet. Something remarkable and distinct happens around the fire and in the presence of Story. A story is not simply a record of an event. A story is a vital and dynamic little world, an ecology, beautiful and inter-connected, that when we enter, makes us whole. In these times of great disarray and alienation, Story has been diminished and forgotten and we are lost as a people and a species without it. Laura Simms has known, since she was a child, that Story is a medicine for our great ailment. She has been telling stories for forty years.

In the past, people of all cultures, everywhere on the earth, gathered together to hear stories for the same reasons they gathered to tell dreams. These narratives contained the wisdom of the culture and the ancestors, they taught the people how to see and live, they opened the paths of vision. One of the essential qualities they reveal is integrity and so it is a given that the value of the story told depends also on the integrity of the storyteller. She must be able to embody the esteemed qualities of the story in her own life, or the story will not be credible. She must know what the story means, and the only way to know this is through living Story in her own life.

The protagonist of a story is cast out, or sets out, from the known or the afflicted place, to do the deed, to seek the gift or vision. Perhaps, at first, she is traveling for her own life, but, ultimately, she will return with the gift that will restore the community. Sometimes she is away for many years because she has to wander among strangers in different lands and cultures for the rare medicine to heal the times. In her parallel story, Laura Simms sets out, seeking, meeting the old women and the old men, the beggars and strangers, the other tale tellers, who may hold the secrets, the ancient map—trying to find her way.

What is she searching for? For the potion, the elixir, the magic formula, that will heal the mysterious ailment, without which we will surely die.

Stories are complex. In the play *Coming from a Great Distance*, by the Traveling Jewish Theater, it is said that "Stories go in circles. They don't go in straight lines." And so it is. And also "...there are stories inside stories and stories between stories and finding your way through them is as easy and as hard as finding your way home."

In *Our Secret Territory*, we are called, as the TJT advises, to "listen in circles," so we can find our way through them, can find our way home.

I don't think Laura Simms was thinking of this, particularly, when she chose to tell stories, stories within, inside and between stories, classic stories, contemporary, yours and mine, while writing about Story itself, while telling the stories of the telling of the stories, and then telling the stories that she has lived, telling this all together in one narrative.

Remember the story of the enchanted brother whose magic shirt lacked a sleeve and so he was restored from a bird to a boy, but with one wing instead of his arm? Laura Simms is a storyteller who has learned that each detail is required for the restoration of the sacred whole. She intimately knows the dance between the text and the improvisation, between the classic rendition and the living event. And so, this book also tells the story of a woman on a journey, being trained, immersing herself in the material, being tested, taking great risks, failing, failing again, trying again, until she, also, comes to the ultimate challenge, struggles, and meets it.

In P.D. Eastman's classic children's story, a baby bird falls out of the nest and wanders around asking, "Are you my mother?" The bird isn't seeking its own mother necessarily, it just needs a mother. It is Laura Simms' long and devoted training as a storyteller that calls her to bring healing to a young ex-child soldier from one of the hells on our planet, Sierra Leone. And when he—not a baby bird who has fallen out of the nest, but a young man stolen out of his village, his childhood, his life, tortured by war—asks "Are you my mother?" Laura Simms' answer confirms that she has become a wise woman who lives the Way. We trust Laura Simms because of the way she lives Story and we trust Story because of the way she lives.

A basic tenet of this beautiful and heart wrenching, heart opening book is that reciprocity, relationship, interchange are essential to Story and its telling. Story emerges out of intact and vital cultures. And the telling of the Story sinks back into the culture, fertilizing it, and so the life force is invigorated. In such times as these, classic stories no longer grow in the desert of our lives. What has been defined as human and meaningful is vanishing rapidly, as rapidly as animal and plant species are becoming extinct.

But comes the Storyteller, a messenger from an old, far world of beauty and meaning. She lights the fire and we gather round, and the stories she tells penetrate our hearts. We are restored; a new culture begins to grow from such seeds.

Story is a medicine. Laura Simms is a great medicine woman and *Our Secret Territory* is the means through which she works her magic for each of us and on behalf of the future.

—Deena Metzger

Introduction

What have you done with the garden
that was entrusted to you?

—Antonio Machado

eMy GARDEN IS THICK; overgrown with stories and memories, encounters and forgetting. Over the last forty years I have become a storyteller. I have been intrigued by the depth and multiplicity of meanings and deep effect that stories heard in presence and reciprocity engender. The best way I have found to articulate something that is more experience than logic, and far more open to discovery than rife with conclusion, is through writing. The chapters in this book are storied conversations, mythic explorations that attempt to provide both a way into the profound realm of living narrative and also a direct sense of what takes place between listener and audience. What occurs in the moment by moment activity of this special listening/seeing is more like a waking dream than a witnessed performance and more akin to spiritual journey than literary event.

As a child growing up in Brooklyn, I loved to crawl alone under the leaves of the hydrangea bush in my back yard and make up stories. I acted them out; sometimes alone and sometimes choreographing dramas with my neighborhood companions. In retrospect, I assume that this passionate endeavor, my oasis of play, was my initial beginnings of becoming a storyteller. My friends would grow weary of the event and I would call out over and over, "Let's go on with the story."

I have no idea of the actual amount of time I spent in play. It comes to my memory as serious, wild and timeless. I entered a landscape of imaginative participation that was ripe with solitude, possibility, and redolent with burgeoning compassion. I played out confrontations between evil and undiluted good, pretending to be a combination Maid Marian and Robin Hood solving the problems of the world. I was born after the Holocaust in a neighborhood of survivors and unspoken stories. Perhaps this place of imagination was how I acknowledged the shadow of death and misery that existed in every house.

In adolescence, stunned by my beautiful mother's crippling stroke, I secreted myself into my bedroom closet with a journal. By then, "the place" became more private and hidden. The magic of words, images, and reflection provided refuge. I wanted to understand how such suffering could occur. It was how I learned to take possession of "our shared secret territory." Here arose my initial taste of what I have come to know as "abiding presence": that which is engendered through the process of storytelling engagement. It was, unknowingly, also my introduction to the nature of mind uncovered and made familiar during meditation practice which began in my early twenties.

My curiosity about storytelling and traditional ritual led me to become a student of a Tibetan Buddhist Meditation teacher. I tasted the potential of storytelling as a penetrating act of compassion as I spent more and more of my free time on retreats at Karme Choling in Vermont. My teacher, Chogyam Trungpa, Rinpoche once said to me, "Don't stop telling fairytales."

Everything that I read about storytelling touched me. However, my quest was to understand what happened between the living audience in the present and me as storyteller. I have gathered reflections on this process from many sources over many years and put them together. I hope that they have the potential to bring alive what takes place and how much benefit occurs from the story responsibly and heartfully told.

The chance to fall under the spell of a spoken story in today's world is becoming increasingly rare. It is impossible for me to imagine how it is to be a child and instantly gain access to digital projected reality without first stabilizing the inner capacity for reflection, discernment and imagination. As a result, as the years have passed, my involvement with storytelling has expanded to the territory of compassionate action. I came more and more to understand that the engagement itself was as potent if not more penetrating than the content of the story on our minds today. It is a way, if a story is told from the heart, to experience inherent inner peace. It is a means of guiding myself and others into and through a journey of awakening that is almost absent from other less dynamic and immediate mediums of communication. This is the engine of my perseverance.

Our Secret Territory is a map that points outward and inwards. It points outward toward a vigorous realignment of our true nature with insight and psychological renewal. It is a subtle and visceral means of setting in motion the natural inner facility to rest the mind in abiding presence beyond thought, and to stimulate awake the intelligence of intuitive imagination that provides us with a fertile pliable mind of kindness and relationship.

My devotion to retelling traditional stories woven with personal narrative has prevailed, as I develop a deeper recognition of the truth known through mythic perspective. And, the vital need to open our "sacred" eyes of perception beyond the limits of literal interpretation.

The chapters are interspersed with short tales, quotes, and poems. These interludes are meant to provoke insight, and to nurture a sense of mystery—to trust that which vanishes when explained. Throughout, a single fairytale unfolds, "Hen and Rooster," winding in and out like a river through cities of stories, offering further clues into the intangible symbolic journey that can connect us with our wholeness and stabilize "that place of inner peace and creativity."

This is not a book about method or analysis; it is a series of invitations to explore my journey, from sensing the power of storytelling to discovering how it can serve as a tool for compassionate service in the world in many challenging situations.

The dynamic collaboration of presence, reciprocity, symbol, language, form, and engagement is bigger than the combination of the parts. Something invaluable manifests that cannot be explained. There is the opportunity of the ongoing event revealing or connecting us with our "Buddha nature," our "noble heart," or as described by Shambhala Buddhist teachings, Basic Goodness—the innate wisdom within us all.

Storytelling provides an immediate relief from self-preoccupation and stress. In this way it is entertainment at its most meaningful. It is a means of urging us into the underworld of presence and wisdom. Hence we are not only inspired by the possibilities of our imagination, but find meaning and value in fresh perception and insight about ourselves and our world. When there is continuous exposure to the templates of transformation provoked by myth and fairytale, epic and enlightened teaching tales, we become haunted by a bigger view of sanity. This renders us stewards of the heart. We are then naturally and joyfully engaged in compassionate action. At its best, whether we are child or adult, we can recover our unyielding connection to the natural world within and without.

The tale of

THE HEN AND THE ROOSTER

begins

THERE was once an aging king whose reign was fraught with troubles and wars. He had three sons. There was no mention of a queen. One day the old king called his two eldest sons before him, offering them the chance to become the ruler in his place on one condition. He asked the eldest, and then the middle son, "Can you build me a place of prayer that has no fault?" Each prince said they could not. So, the old king called his youngest son and asked him the same question. The youngest prince responded, "Yes, I can."

The young prince sought advice and teachings from the most famous architects, carpenters, artists, scientists and scholars of his time. They helped him design a faultless building. When it was constructed, not a single person found fault with it.

But just as the king was about to enter the door and place the crown on his youngest son's head, an old man passed by. The old man looked at the building and remarked, "It is beautiful on the outside, but the foundation is uneven." He had seen what no one else could see.

It's time to see by a different light,

It's time to turn on the moon.

—NANCY WILLARD

Crossing into the Invisible

How the Storyteller Guides Us into an Unseen Realm

There was an orphan boy whose job it was to watch the freshly-threshed corn on the threshing floor of the barn. One day he fell asleep and the hens ate the corn. His stepmother was furious. He exclaimed, "But I had a remarkable dream. I was standing with one foot in this world and one foot in the other. The sun was on my right side and the moon was on my left. I wore a crown and my body was speckled with stars."

"Give me that dream," demanded the stepmother.

"I cannot. It is my dream," he answered. "It came and it went."

Angrily, she sent him away. He stepped over the threshold and went out into the world in search of his fortune.

*I*N THE LITERAL STORY, the threshold the dreamer crossed was the barn and the life that he knew. In a more secret sense, the threshold was the dreamer himself, who would not give away his dream. The hidden jewel is the storytelling, wherein the listener crosses over the threshold that separates the waking mind from the invisible world within. To bring an audience into an abiding present is as significant and far-reaching as understanding the narrative text or the psychological travels instigated by a story's images. It is what awakens us and lets us step again and again over the threshold of our own limited perceptions.

Our journey into the chapters of this book begins with these two young men, an orphan and a youngest prince, who leave what they know behind to go out into the world.

Writing about performance, Peter Brook says, "The essential thing is to recognize that there is an invisible world that needs to be made visible."[1] The experience of being swept into the ritual of ongoing story teaches us that the ground of the visible world is the invisible world out of which it arises.

As the characters in the fairytale cross thresholds into other realms, we listeners are drawn inward past the boundaries of our logical minds into vast space and communal presence. The words beguile our minds with profuse detail as our imaginations recreate the story. The habitual patterns of thinking that usually patrol the borders of this familiar world are engaged, and thus the door falls open inward—we feel the ever-present timeless space of mind that has always existed beneath consciousness.

The teller frees us to dream awake. "We must pass through dreams in order to perceive the supernatural dimensions of the natural," writes Helene Cixous.[2] The story and the telling provide doorways to be opened. The process of telling provides the push that sends us across.

The first doorway opens onto the threshold of longing. Then, we cross the threshold of no return followed by the unrelenting threshold of death. In the middle of the journey we sink through the threshold of mystery until we ascend again over the threshold of return.

The threshold of longing: From the moment the storyteller begins to speak, our attention is focused by his or her presence and voice and by the beginning of the story. We hover half in and half out of our world, longing to find out more about the world of the story. If the voice is trustworthy, we shift our attention seemingly outward, while setting the ground for an inner visualization. A Turkish storyteller's proverb says, "The voice is half the wisdom." And the tale itself slowly seduces our minds into wanting to know what is going to happen next...

> The Dreamer came to a palace. The King was outside and inquired what he was doing. The boy explained how he had lost his home and work because of his dream. "Give me your dream!" ordered the King. When the boy refused he was placed in a dungeon.

> But the princess, who was being forced to marry a king that she mistrusted, took pity on the Dreamer and brought him food. Night after night he solved impossible riddles posed by her father until he won her freedom. At last she was married to the Dreamer, which caused the rejected king to declare war upon their Kingdom. The Dreamer said, "I will battle the king" and went off to fight without an army. He was armed with his dreaming mind.

Moved forward by the storyteller's living voice, we construct a basic landscape within which the characters of the story can perform without constant reconstruction. We are moved to inquire about what will happen next. The longing opens our hearts with a different kind of desire. This is the passage over the first threshold.

Such longing is akin to entering the grounds that surround a sacred temple, a place where one will have the opportunity to come face to face with the Divine: the pilgrim "is within a temenos, or precinct, a place 'cut off' from the common land and dedicated to a god."[3] The threshold of no return is both a state of mind and an uninterrupted involvement in the co-creation of the narrative. Longing releases our discursive mind while imagination rises up from the heart and inner eye to conduct the unfolding drama of the story.

The listener is literally carried away—it is as if a little trap door in the inner world falls open, and we hardly notice that our listening activity is propelled onward like a natural waterfall.

We would be disappointed and disturbed if we were to be interrupted. What is it that holds us so fast? Beneath the response to the spoken narrative, the natural space of mind rests in a vast ocean of silence that is reassuringly familiar and wholesome. "The door opens," as Cixous tells us of stories, "directly into the soul."

Another example of catapulting across the threshold of no return is exemplified in The Tale of The Warrior Princess. An eldest and a middle brother took up the challenge of a foreign princess who swore to marry whatever man could defeat her in single combat. Who would not want to know what was going to happen next?

Each brother traveled over seven mountain ranges, and each came to an old man standing alone in a valley. The old man said, "Tell me, what do you value most, advice from me or rushing off to battle the princess?" Each brother refused his advice, saying, "I don't need an old man's advice. I am going to marry the princess." Each brother was beheaded in the battle, bedazzled by the armored warrior who tricked them by baring her breasts just as the battle began.

When the third and youngest prince rode out, we, like him, are prepared to take the old man's advice:

"She is not strong. She tricks those who meet her heedlessly. When she lifts her spear to start the battle, look away and do not be distracted."

The wisdom of the old man reflects our inner state of knowing, as well as the composure in listening that supports the audience. Later we learn that her ruse of baring her breasts is not as magnetizing as opening the heart.

The threshold of death awaits us all. There is no avoiding it, and the story allows us to taste its insistence.

In a Norwegian fairytale, the hero came to a crossroads where there were three signs: "He who travels down this road will return unharmed"; "He who travels this path may or may not return";

and "He who travels here will never return." Of course, he chose the third. How else would we discover the outcome of this journey? But it is just a story—and we are not aware that the characters, the feeling, the landscape, and the task are created by ourselves, since we have crossed over into the becoming of everything with no return. The road imagined is ours. The fear felt is conjured from our own experience.

> He met a wolf whose body was so thin from hunger that his ribs shone through his fur like crystals. The starving beast said, "If you feed me, I will take you where you have to go." The prince replied, "But I have no food myself."
>
> The wolf howled pitifully, "Then kill the horse you ride on and let me eat your beast." Having come this far, the youth, weeping, killed his horse and fed it to the wolf. The wolf took him across the uncrossable border of his father's kingdom to the realm of a heartless giant.

In the invisible world of our inner drama we have killed our only conscious vehicle of travel, our sweetest companion, and passed over the threshold of death. Here, in the exercise of imagination, we murder the safe path, killing our own limited means of travel. What is most terrible or feared must be done in the mind to meet our terror and contain it in our waking lives. The vastness of listening contains all the fear of the universe.

The hero or heroine sometimes dies and is reborn, like the shaman who sheds his skin and loses his bones to journey to the other world to retrieve health, lost souls, or information unavailable to us. We, too, in hearing shift our allegiance from the ways of this world to a magical listening that arises from the mind before thought emerges. We let go of our expectations and preconceptions, defying all logic in our pilgrimage toward the end of the story.

The threshold of mystery: having crossed so far, we no longer question the logic of the story or spring back into conceptual thinking. We are committed to going forward with the events because they are of our own making. All the while, we sink deeper

A youngest prince discovered that his two sisters had disappeared in a super-natural whirlwind before his birth. He set off to find them. He refused his father's army and wealth, instead taking only a harp that had no strings, which he had found in the basement. He learned to play it.

His music was stunning, and all who heard him wept for joy. He tricked demons and stupefied monsters, winning a cloak of invisibility.

into the sensuousness of total presence. The experience is of a lush inner relaxation, familiar and vast. No one thinks about it while it is happening because to think about it would be to lose it. Later it is called enchantment or trance. But it is wide awake.

The journey of this prince crossed four worlds, and our imagination goes with him freely. He traveled in uncanny ways, beyond conception or visibility, to the incomprehensible realm of the Queen of Everything, who had turned her back on our world. Her island was surrounded by hundreds of thousands of warriors. Their spears held the heads of everyone who had attempted to pass into her garden by conventional means or force.

The prince put on his cloak of invisibility and entered the Queen's garden. He saw twenty white doves fly to earth and turn into twenty women, and in the center stood the Queen. Without thinking, he took off his cloak, revealing himself, and called her name. He no longer cared if he lived or died.

The opening of the heart without fear takes place in the crossing of this threshold. We have learned to alight and ascend from a groundless place, trusting that we contain all possibilities. Needless to say, we are held by the presence of the storyteller, our guide on this holy excursion, although each of us enters the temple of our own design.

The Queen was taken by surprise. "How did you get here?" she inquired. The prince told his entire story, and she invited him to dine with her. "I will allow you to enter into my palace because you came with a good heart and did not attempt to enter with force."

It is not surprising that we who listen to stories do not want the tale to end at this point. To remain in the garden of the Queen, to enter her palace, is the culmination of the journey— one that is most pleasurable, with none of our everyday concerns of rent and worry, responsibilities or illness, death and loss. Her palace is not described.

The threshold of return is necessary and most poignant. The storyteller knows the story will soon end and in a thousand unspoken ways is gently preparing us for re-entry, holding the reins of attention while letting out its taut line slowly—by sound of voice, by intention, by the knowledge that our lives are social, responsible, and that the story event was only the practice. How we live our ordinary lives is what is essential.

In truth, the storyteller knows that the timelessness found in listening is always the ground of all existence. And the true challenge to the listener, and to the storyteller, is to acknowledge this in waking life.

In the most moving of Scottish fairytales, the hero Diarmud ("No Envy") passed through three worlds and gave up everything to save his dying otherworldly wife. He went where no man had ever gone to retrieve the Cup that Heals. However, as he was about to offer her the drink, a red dwarf appeared:

> "I forgot to tell you that when she finishes the drink you will not love her any more. Do not pretend. She will know. The king will hold a celebration in his world beneath the sea. Accept no gift. Ask only for a ship to return to your world."

> When he offered her the drink that would save her life, the love left his heart. She saw it and withdrew.

> When he sailed back to his companions and all the people of the world, they awaited him on the shore with great joy. They had feared that he, greatest hero and poet, lover of the feminine and hunter of the sacred, who alone had crossed three thresholds into other worlds, would stay in the other world forever. And we would have been left without his story.

. . .

The prince who played the harp that had no strings returned to his world to free his sisters from wrathful forces of the supernatural and became a great king. He understood the intricate relationship between nature and human beings and how it had fallen out of balance. He also knew the necessity for the queen to be part of our world in all her power.

• • •

And the Dreamer traveled back to his wife after five years. The old king had died, and she sat the Dreamer on the throne. Because of his journey, one foot was planted in each world. She sat beside him like the sun, the other king's daughter sat beside him like the moon, and the water from a golden bowl his five-year-old son held shimmered on his chest like the stars in the sky. "You did not give away your dream and it has come true," said the queen.

The storyteller returns us to our ordinary perceptions, letting us come back gently: "And so the story ends and they all lived happily ever after."

This lie that we will all live happily ever after is a lie only in a world concerned solely with the visible. For knowing that the invisible world is ever-present and ever-nourishing in the visible world, we do indeed live happily ever after, regardless of the ceaseless manifestations of the world and the truth of death.

The real journey of these spoken fairytales takes us to a place that does not exist but must be reached, and then brings us back again. Like the heroine or hero adorned with wisdom and story, we bring back a secret treasure of awareness that is priceless. For the stepping over is a "seeing, as the Hindu would say, the darshan...the viewing of the sacred itself."[4] The story ends like a pilgrimage, having brought us to the inner chamber in the temple where one might view a statue of a deity or discover nothing at all. The journey was the crossing.

THE HEN AND THE ROOSTER

continues...

THE youngest prince had the building torn down and he began again. He constructed an even more beautiful and carefully built tower. He had a "church" erected with a perfect foundation. Not a single person found fault with it, until the same old man happened by.

He threw up his hands. "What a pity that such an apparently impeccable building was built with a crooked tower." He sighed and walked away. The prince had the second temple demolished.

The descent into the depths will bring healing.

C. G. JUNG

What Storytelling Means to Me

*W*HEN I SET OUT to become a storyteller, 1968, there were no maps, charts, or recognizable destinations that defined a career. I was following an invisible thread, as if seen in a dream half-remembered. It remains a labor of love. The vividness, aliveness, directness, and endless challenge I felt then still inspire me. No matter how simple a story I choose (or chooses me), it is like a multifaceted diamond revealed in the telling that I can never quite fathom. The quest continues. My unquenchable faith in basic goodness and mystery is nourished.

In these sentences lie some of my answers. The past and the present are connected in the act of performance. For me, storytelling is more ritual than entertainment, more reciprocal event than solo show where I have a starring role. I respect and honor these qualities of what I have chosen to do. I enjoy them. I feel relieved to engage in a life's work that continuously benefits people and makes me more human, humble, and responsive.

When I first wrote this it was 1986. I am rewriting it in 2009. I have learned enough to call myself a storyteller and to begin and begin again each time, feet planted on the earth, spine straight, quite confident that I can spontaneously tell a story directly to my audience, letting it flow. The story tells itself; I hear it as it is spoken. I feel it come to life through my listener.

My first real interest in storytelling arose from my regard for the potency and healing qualities of ritual in traditional cultures, my love for anthropology, literature, psychology, spirituality, world music, poetry, dance, and great drama. How could I choose what I wanted to do for my future? I kept searching for an answer.

No answers, but experiences occurred; manifesting coincidences which only appear related and connected in hindsight. I told a Russian fairytale by accident April 15, 1968 in front of the Hans Christian Andersen statue in Central Park. An elderly woman passing by heard me. She asked me to tell stories there in the summer months. I agreed. She turned out to be the Baroness Dahlerup, who had sat on Andersen's knees when she was six years old. A week later I was invited, again a seeming accident, to view a film at the American Museum of Natural History of a Blackfoot woman healing someone with a physical illness through incanting a sacred myth. The next day, I volunteered to tell fairytales at the Children's Aid Society. Listeners of all ages, everyone startled into enchantment, kept asking me for more stories. I wanted to know more about what oral storytelling means, and I still do. I wanted to comprehend what happened between me and the audience.

I began constructing dance dramas, stories, and poems when I was seven years old. I began to "play" telling stories both as a solo event and as a narrator in a dance drama recounting ancient myths that we performed in parks throughout New York City.

When I was twenty, my mother died. She left me her diamond ring in her will. It was given to her by her mother, who had brought it from Romania. I do not know the history of the ring before that time. She wore it to formal events, and to cook and garden. However, my father's new wife, a veritable wicked stepmother, hid it from me. I dreamed of the ring and stole it. For twenty years after my mother's death, I kept it in a safe deposit box in the bank. Then I began to wear it just as my mother did. It is a deceptive ring. Its seemingly flat surface is encased in white gold. It is very beautiful, but few people recognize its value monetarily or personally. When I held it beneath a magnifying glass there was a world within a world within a world of crystal rooms, each one revealing the other. It seemed to go on forever. Five years ago, I left it in a box in my bathroom during a ten day visit of nine Bhutanese monks performing in New York. Strangers came in and out of my house during that time. Afterwards I found the ring was gone.

This precious ring is like my storytelling. I had stolen it when guided by a dream in which my mother appeared and showed me where it was. I had to let go of the ring, the outer connection to my mother and ideas of my possessions, and trust that what I lost was always to be found within.

. . .

Everything that I care about is practiced and honored in the performance, in the teaching, the recording, and study related to this art-form. Yet, I am always aware of how little I actually do know about the profound ways in which language, energy, and sound function between us to heal in this world.

Looking back I am grateful that teachers have appeared in my life to keep me (most of the time) from inflation and fixation. As soon as I thought I knew what I was doing, that surety was swept away. Listening has become the key to opening the door that leads to room within room of the stories I tell, or the stories I am told.

I am constantly provoked by the importance of storytelling in our lives at present. Through the fortunate event of meeting a Tibetan Buddhist meditation teacher, I have attempted to break down concepts about what stories mean and how they heal, to go beyond what I assumed and find ways to instigate enduring change at a deeper level. My most demanding task has been to discover what it might mean to be an unbiased listener.

. . .

I know that the story I am telling is not the story that my audiences are hearing or imagining. Everyone hears their own tale with their own images, associations, and life experiences. How humbling, how humorous, how like the world itself. It was humbling to feel that I could become deities and heroines, and accept that I was conduit and not god. The center of the event is presence, a tent pole holding up a gossamer screen, like a Javanese shadow puppet performance. In the best events, all things arise and vanish moment by moment.

I study a great deal. There are many disciplines that have carved their teachings into my tattooed body: mindfulness awareness practice; observation and self-investigation to explore characterization; open voice to embody the story in the telling; yoga for flexibility and also for fluidity; research into the ways cultures see story; psychological meaning and not being attached to those meanings; the possibilities of conflict resolution to provide a ground for new dialogue; and on and on. Side by side with that has been a practice in improvisation, listening, accepting the unforeseen and surprising turns, hearing something new from my own voice, enjoying the enjoyment of my audience and giving it away. I am funnier. My timing has improved and I don't take myself as seriously as I did long ago. I am no longer attached to the deep feelings evoked by the story in myself, so it is more penetrating for others to feel more. I am exposed, and not, usually, embarrassed by mistakes.

Storytelling is a one person show, but it is reciprocal. I love to construct the whole concert and then to change things, hanging a journey on having an unspoken thread throughout. Eighteen years ago I began an experiment weaving true life in and out of ancient myth and it has been a marvelous revelation of the meaning and significance of myth in our ordinary lives. We are living story all the time, and guided by invisible tales we tell ourselves. I personally set out to use myself as a guinea pig and unstick the inner tale I was telling. Where was I stuck in my own fairytale? How can I, dare I, help anyone else before doing this?

How we tell a story makes the difference since the same content can either fix our minds on a single interpretation or open our minds, liberate us from grasping, into multiple awareness.

Wim Wenders, a filmmaker, explores story in his films. I read an essay he wrote, in which he said that all stories are lies but we cannot live without them. It made clear something I knew but couldn't say. It helped me to understand my growing respect and love for storytelling. All stories *are* lies. They are what we do with information, with events, with other stories. They live at the moment when they are being told. They hold together jewels of images, like beads on a string. The images slide down into us unseen, releasing more images, meaning, and feelings... unlocking the door to other worlds within...unhinging the discursive mind's fixation and fertilization of the field of being. The story itself may not be true, although it reveals truth moment by moment. We do it as fluidly as we breathe.

An old aboriginal man told the story of creation: one person is always dreaming another person dreaming and another person dreaming.

The result of this act of "deep-see" listening and telling can be a settled mind, a renewed clarity of vision, which allows us to live our own story in the world of nature's story with more responsibility, poignantly—with respect for others, and humor, compassion, and meaning. That is why I am still becoming a storyteller.

Dreams, his mother said, are only stories:

except they aren't stories like the ones in books.

Dreams are your own stories, inside...each one nested

within all the others....Stories are what history not

made of time is made of.

— JOHN CROWLEY, *Aegypt*

Summoning the Realm of Dream

From over the entrance, they say, came the neighing of horses.
From the other side too came the neighing of horses, they say.
"Something's happened! Wake up!"
"People have heard something wonderful here."
— Robert Bringhurst, *Everywhere Being Is Dancing*

*W*HETHER OR NOT WE remember our own night dreams, we all agree that they occur. But the memory of the dream is always a tale told—a shadow of the actual dream, whose complexity is beyond the grasp of the waking mind. These dreams happen and are experienced in a timeless present that our waking mind cannot hold in its sense-making allegiance to time and understanding.

Many contemporary researchers believe, as do all traditional peoples, that the realm of dreaming is not limited to sleep. Dreaming mind pervades and feeds our daytime lives, it is said, like an underground river flowing beneath conscious thinking. This timeless place beyond history, which is ongoing in the present, keeps fresh the unseen root system of our logical minds. Every time a story is told and heard, the channel to the realm of dreams is opened and the dreamer within is summoned. The listener's dreaming mind awakens, provoked by sound and breath, word and image.

There are different kinds of dreams. There are significant dreams that seem to rearrange our daily lives and there are more ordinary dreams that seem to have less urgent meaning for us— almost as if they are part of the cleansing system of the psyche.

And then there are dreams, night or day, like visions, what are often called Big Dreams. Marc Barasch, author of *Healing Dreams*, discussed these kinds of vivid, startling, sometimes life shifting dreams with a Choctaw friend named Preston. "He said, 'You always have a choice. If you have a big dream and don't want to follow it, well, then, you can leave it alone. But that's when you start to go blind. You go into the dark world. You make the same circle again and again, the same routine day in and day out. If you follow your dream, humbly, that is where your real life begins.'"[1]

I want to talk, therefore, about dreaming—not as the unconscious activity that occurs when we sleep, but as the natural process of being. We share this realm of dreams, which the Australian Aborigines call the Dream Time, Alcheringa, with all the people of the world and all of nature. This realm is not a place identifiable in time or space, nor is it a concept that can be described—unless we speak in stories, in poems, in metaphor or song. Only in these ways can the layered levels of simultaneous occurrences and infinite possibilities be experienced directly.

According to Sioux elders, "When the world was coming into being there was song before words. That's why music heals us. We all have the memory of this first language."

Tibetan scholar Namkhai Norbu has written a text about his search for the Bon roots of Tibetan religion.[2] He wrote of the oral Tibetan stories: "They were instruments for the discovery of wisdom which could not be communicated, 'keys' to open the door of knowledge of the ineffable and the unknown."

The following summary of a fairytale offers an experience in language that permits both intuitive dreaming mind and logical mind to listen concurrently.

There was once a king who went blind. His body grew weak. When his three sons wanted to heal him, he sent them to find fruit from the garden of the Queen of Everything. The two oldest princes each went alone, only to have the same experience. Arriving at the end of seven mountain ranges beyond an iceberg they saw an old man who was sewing up the cracks in the earth that had split because it was too dry.

The two sons each wished the old man ill fortune. His activity made no sense to them. The old man wished them ill fortune in return. Neither son found the Queen's garden, although they journeyed far.

Then the youngest son set out. He came upon the same old man. He wished the old man well. The old man wished him well and gave him detailed instructions about how to find the garden and acquire the fruit. The youngest son obeyed and discovered the fruit. Just as he was about to take the fruit home to heal his father, he was overtaken by intense longing to see the Queen herself. He entered her tower and found her asleep. Deeply moved by her beauty he kissed her cheek three times without waking her and left. He returned home with the fruit and gave it to the King. However the King was not healed. The next day, the Queen awoke. Seeing the marks on her cheek, she rode out with seven armies (she ruled seven kingdoms) to discover who had stolen the fruit and kissed her. The youngest prince told the true story of how he had crossed into her territory, found the fruit and kissed her three times. She healed the King and commanded that the youngest prince marry her. Which he did, gladly.

The true fruit was her *magic* knowledge. She then ruled seven kingdoms plus one. Let me describe the Queen as she is spoken of in this marvelous fairytale from the Caucasus:

> She slept on a golden bed. On her brow she had a star and under her shoulder the moon shone out. Her waist could be spanned by two fingers, but if one let her go, she would fill the whole world. Gold and silver lamps stood at her head and at her feet.[3]

She is impossible, beyond logic. However she is the possibility of the dreaming mind unlimited by lack of imagination and a self-centered viewpoint (the two older sons' unwillingness to recognize the actual meaningfulness of the old man's work). She is the peacemaker, the healer, the knowing that is needed to sit equally beside the King to truly fulfill rulership.

The youngest son, the fresh perspective, the least controlled by opinions of who he is and the world around him, saw the old man and did not discredit his worth because what he was doing was unknown to him. He did not denigrate what was unfamiliar and made no waking sense. He alone discovered the palace of the Queen, the realm of intuitive mind and heart, entered her garden and her chamber; the place of refreshment, the place of healing.

All fairytales and spiritual quests are in search of consecrating this marriage within. Once wed, the desert of reason, without imagination and heart, becomes moist and fertile once again. The need to control, to be right, is replaced by creative listening and thinking, good humor, and wisdom that manages situations and sees its own opinions as just that—simply opinions.

The storyteller can be seen in this light as the medium who reconnects us to the dreamer within ourselves, a dreamer already connected to all the peoples that have ever been and the natural world that we share. The listening is then a form of initiation. Anthropologist Victor Turner says in *The Forest of Symbols* that

"Initiation is not a matter of transferring a capacity, but of revealing that which is already there in potential."[4]

Tradition is far more than the sharing of stories, or the preservation of museum artifacts. Tradition is the continuity of pathways that access inherent creativity and wisdom. What we risk losing is the knowledge of how to keep open the channel to the dream. It is a responsibility and one of the important functions of the storyteller to keep the dreaming wide awake.

The storyteller is a mnemonic device to remind us that all day we are constructing tales of how we would like to see our past, what we think we are doing in the present, and how we fantasize it will be in the future. This is the activity of our thinking minds. Thinking thoughts like endless clouds shifting shapes in open sky. The more attached we become to the constructions, the less available the world of dream, the world of mediation and abundance.

Recognizing the dreamer wide awake gives birth to a sense of joy, humor, renewal and an increase in meaning and compassion. Telling stories then connects us to the history that exists where no time occurs and prepares us to live fully in the history we are making, moment by moment, into the future.

HOW DOES DREAMING MANIFEST IN STORYTELLING?

Meaning. The hidden interior light that makes things, the light which casts a matching shadow in the mind, picture, a glyph: not a picture of its shape or size or color, not a sign of its difference from me but of its likeness to me: of its Meaning. A glyph combinable with others in a language hot enough, powerful enough, to dissolve the distance between Inside and Outside, the fountain and the mirror, strong enough to replace the thing with its Meaning. To make wishes come true.

—*Aegypt,* JOHN CROWLEY

1. Listeners do not hear the story that I tell. They envision their own stories, created in the process of listening, adorned by the imagery, associations, and feelings evoked by their own dreaming minds. The listeners' images are provoked by the storyteller's words, but they do not come from outside. The images arise from each listener. Each person's story, each time it is heard, is totally unique and fresh.

2. The story heard, like the dream dreamed, is remembered only in an edited retelling of a more personal version. It is experienced in the moment of the telling, but impossible to fully recall because it cannot be held by words or concepts alone. Like the incongruous description of the Queen, or Jesus' Kingdom of Heaven in a mustard seed, whole universes fit on the tip of a needle.

3. This imagining provides us with endless creative possibilities and fresh insights and ways of perceiving. It delights the mind. The logical mind in union with the intuition is refreshed. The story in the listening is the meaning. The analysis or memory is always limited.

No matter what sort of story is told, when it is heard in the reciprocity of the performance, the tale heard is not possible. Impossible because the listener becomes everything in the story: the landscape, all the characters, the weather, objects described and not described, things visible and invisible, moment by moment. A plethora of images arises from the slimmest evocation. A phantasm of pictures one upon another appears in no space, unbound by time, couched in silence like the hidden images in ancient caves that have not yet been discovered. The teller and the listener become the old man sewing together the cracks in the dry earth—binding the separation between the unconditional mind of open sky dream and the earth bound mind we often assume is all there is.

Everything that is

Is alive

The lantern walks around

The wall of this house has its own true home

The antlers on the graves rise and circle the mounds

While the dead themselves get up and

Go visit the

living ones.

—SHAMAN'S SONG,
translated by David Cloutier

Seeing the Invisible

*M*ANY YEARS AGO A Chippewa Cree storyteller told my dear friend anthropologist Frances Harwood what an elder said to her: "Don't mourn the loss of our stories. Someone will make them up again."

This statement disturbed me, yet something about it felt true. Only recently did I begin to understand the profundity and wisdom of this teaching. One has to look within the words, inside their obvious meaning, to find their truest sense. Beneath the traditional interpretation is the wellspring of wisdom. It is our task to find that route again.

Let me tell you a story from the Kikuyu of Kenya. I have loved this story and told it for many years. The first telling was in New Zealand to a Maori audience. When I finished, an old woman and elder, a *kuia*, said, "You are telling stories to call your ancestors back to you."

On that same trip, a Maori chief explained that when stories are properly told and heard, when ceremonies are done correctly, when we live in harmony with one another, with ourselves and with the earth, the seeds in each of us in the House of Treasures are set vibrating.

....

There was once a man who had black and white cows. He tended them as if they were his children. Every day he took the cows to green pastures to graze. One morning he found their udders empty. They gave no milk. He took them further to greener pastures, but for two more mornings, the cows gave no milk. Their udders were withered and empty and dry. He knew something was wrong.

On the third morning he decided to stay awake all night to watch the cows. And he did. In the middle of the night he saw a rope come down from the sky. Climbing down he saw three beautiful women, star people, carrying calabashes. They placed their gourds on the earth and milked the black and white cows.

The man no longer cared about the precious milk, because these women were so beautiful. He wanted to marry one. He caught her. She struggled. He held her tight while the other women rushed back up to the sky. She resisted. She fought him, until finally he said, "Woman, I want to marry you."

She stopped struggling. "I will marry you on one condition," she warned. "I have a finely woven basket. If you promise never to look inside until I give you permission, I will be your wife."

He happily agreed. She married him. She placed her basket by the door of their house. The star woman was a good wife. She even tended his black and white cows.

As time passed, however, the man grew more and more curious about what was in the basket, until he began to think, "She is my wife. Doesn't that mean it is my basket too? What harm will it be if I just look inside?"

One day while she was out with the cows, he decided to look. He slowly opened the basket. To his surprise there was nothing in it. He laughed out loud. "Why did she make such a fuss over nothing!" He closed the basket.

A few minutes later she arrived home asking, "What did you do today?"

"I looked in the basket," he answered boldly.

"What did you see in the basket?" she asked softly.

"What was there to see?" he boasted. "There is nothing in the basket."

"Oh. You saw nothing. But everything is in the basket. All the beautiful things of the sky for you and me. If you would have waited, I would have taught you to see. Now I must go." The woman who came from the sky took her basket and went back to the sky.

....

The Kikuyu storyteller added, "It is the same today; mankind still thinks the things of the spirit are empty."[6]

> The hunger for stories is considerable. People are starving for them. The reason stories are not listened to is that the story making is not a rational process. You can't go to school, as people pretend, and learn how to write a story. You can't learn it because it comes out of the totality of the human spirit.
>
> —Sir Laurens Van der Post

Believing in a story is like sitting on a one-legged milking stool. It needs us as much as we need it.

—TED CHAMBERLAIN

THE HEN AND THE ROOSTER

continues...

FOR the third time the prince built a temple. It was an even more impressive building with a magnificent and precisely constructed tower. As before, not a single person found fault with it until the same old man came by.

He threw up his hands. "It is nearly perfect, but it lacks a rooster and a hen."

This time the king's son left the building standing and announced he would leave the kingdom in search of the rooster and the hen. Disappointed, the old king gave him a three-legged horse and sent him away.

For since there is no fortitude similar to patience

Surely I should put that into practice

—SHANTIDEVA

The Secret Practice

O KNOW PATIENCE IS to come home to the wide-open ears and eyes of unbiased presence. But while patience is the goal of the journey, restraint is the path itself. To remember again and again to pull back from reaction—to wait—strengthens the capacity of the mind to break habitual patterns of intolerance, anger, and hatred. We discover the ability of our heart and mind to rest naturally, regardless of circumstance, and we are weaned from harming both ourselves and others. Restraint gives birth to a trust in oneself and the world so that in the end we can finally fall in love, even with our enemies.

Listening to a story is a secret practice of this path. As we listen to the hero or heroine's adventure, we are tricked into the very experience we so often avoid or are unable to achieve. The dynamic engagement in the story, the mutual seduction of image and emptiness conjured between listener and teller, lures us into an experience of inner tasks as demanding as those of the characters in the tale. We have to wait along with the stubborn or over-zealous hero or heroine as they make the same mistake once again, too quickly react with aggression, or simply fall asleep at the wrong time. Through it all we unwittingly recommit to listen further, and our expectation of quick-fix solutions is undercut as we settle down for yet another episode. The Russian tale of "The Snake Princess" is one among many in which we discover along with the hero that our obstacle-ridden journey is no detour at all but rather one that finally brings us home.

Once a soldier returning home from a battle entered a forest and became lost. He wandered for three days and three nights without rest until he came to a clearing. In its center, a high mound of golden hay reached above the trees. "If I could rest here for exactly one hour, surely I would find my way," the soldier assured himself. He dismounted, leaned back against the hay, and lit his pipe so he would wake in one hour. Exactly on time, he rose and walked to his horse. But he did not notice a single burning ember fall to the ground from his pipe.

He had not ridden far when the haystack burst into flames. He turned to see a woman, encircled by fire, calling out, "Soldier, save me!" He answered, "I have seen too much death. I fear I will be burned." The woman said, "Then thrust your sword into the flames and I will save myself."

Shielding his eyes, the soldier extended his sword. He did not see her turn into a snake, slither along the blade, and crawl up his arm to wrap around his neck seven times. When she took her tail in her mouth and he felt her cold skin, he wailed, "Leave me!" But the snake hissed, "If you keep me around your neck for seven years, I will be a woman again, and you will know bliss." Without hesitation, the soldier agreed. She explained that if he could find the copper palace where she was under an enchantment, held prisoner by a dragon, she could become a princess again, and she would be his wife. He traveled for seven years without finding the palace.

The story becomes our guide. While we are hoping that the soldier and the snake will be saved we fail to notice that it is we who are being rescued. The tale holds us in chains of complicit surrender as the images transform the unfolding events into our own. The image of the woman burning on a haystack causes the soldier to forget his urgent longing for home; and at the same time causes us to forego our attachment to what we know as reality in favor of what cannot be real outside of our own minds. In this way our destiny is, for the moment, entwined with the impatient soldier, the horse he rides on, and the enchanted snake around his throat. His successes and failures become ours. We learn with him that without the patience born from waiting, we cannot return home from battle, from the devastation of war, or the delusion of our unending struggles to attain security.

> On the last day of the seventh year, the soldier saw a steep mountain. On its peak was a copper palace. His horse climbed straight upward as the gates of the palace opened. The snake unwound from the soldier's neck and instantly, touching the earth, turned back into a woman. The soldier sighed in relief. But she said, "If you can remain in the palace for seven days without crossing the threshold, the dragon will be defeated and I can marry you." The soldier said happily, "What is seven days compared with seven years!" Taking the horse to a stable, the princess departed.
>
> The court of the palace was splendid, and the soldier took off his well-worn boots and said out loud, "I could stay here for a hundred years without walking across the threshold. But what is a man to eat?" A copper cask rolled into the room and poured out an abundance of food and drink. When he was full, the cask swallowed what was left and rolled from the room again. In this way, the soldier passed six days. But on the seventh day he began to think, "I am about to marry a princess, and what do I, a soldier, have to offer?" He decided to steal the copper cask. He called out, "I am hungry." In rolled the cask, and he grabbed it in his hands, but it fell to the ground and rolled over the threshold.
>
> Without hesitation, the soldier chased it out the door. Then he heard a sound like thunder and the sky darkened. The copper palace turned to dust, and the dragon, with the princess on its back, flew over the mountain. She called out, "Soldier, if you love me, find the dragon's cave and free me." And she was gone.

The soldier's horse whinnied and came forth from where the stable had stood. He climbed on its back and rode down the mountain, heart aching, saying, "Horse of my heart, let us find the princess."

How difficult it is to practice restraint! And how is it possible to learn the difference between rigidly holding back, becoming paralyzed with fearful hesitation, and skillfully reining in the mind's habits with full awareness? The story gives us the opportunity to explore antidotes, intricacies, and traps. Paradoxically, we make the journey confident that it is not happening to us while at the same time our imaginative and emotional involvement in the telling makes us the only field upon which the story is played out. Protected, we are being prepared for meeting similar situations within ourselves and our own lived existence.

After a long search with no luck, the soldier entered a forest and met an old man leaping up and down upon his own beard. Certain he would have no answer, the soldier asked him if he knew where the cave of the dragon could be found. The old man said he knew and did not know. But he offered his sword of might in exchange for the copper cask and some directions, and the soldier agreed. The old man warned, "Use this sword to destroy only that which needs to be destroyed." He told the soldier that only the witch Baba Yaga, sister to the dragon, could lead him to the cave. "And where do I find Baba Yaga?" asked the seeker. But the old man did not answer.

Entering another forest, the soldier was pursued by a she-bear. When he drew out his sword, she said, "Spare my life and I will help you." Accustomed now to the unusual events on his journey, he agreed. A golden fish frightened him in a stream. She also asked for her life to be spared, and again the soldier did not kill her. Then a falcon landed, darkening the soldier's path and startling him, and he pulled his sword. But the falcon too begged for his life in exchange for his help, and for a third time the soldier agreed. And on he traveled.

In a third forest, Baba Yaga the witch appeared, flying in her metal bowl. She dared the soldier to follow her and flew into the sky. First, she crossed an uncrossable ocean, leaving the soldier in despair, until he remembered the golden fish. The fish became a crystal bridge for him to cross. In pursuit of the witch again, he succumbed to hopelessness as she soared above an impassable mountain. This time the falcon came to his rescue. Once more finding the witch, he followed her until he arrived before a forest so thickly grown that he could not enter, and in utter frustration he watched her fly away over the trees. The she-bear appeared and cleared a path for him. But on the other side of the forest the witch was nowhere to be seen, and a vast plain spread before the soldier as far as his eyes could see.

The she-bear bid him wait while she went to a river to drink, and then she warned him, "This plain is a place where even heroes cannot stay awake. Beware and do not fall asleep. Good luck." Traveling slowly across a lifeless desert covered with the bones of those who had failed, the soldier and the horse grew drowsy. When the man could not hold his head up any longer and the horse was already snoring, with his last strength the soldier pulled out some snuff and placed it in his nostrils. He sneezed loudly, waking the horse and himself, and they crossed the ceaseless plain.

But the cave that they found on the other side was closed with iron stones, and the soldier came to a halt.

In the telling of this tale, nearly forty minutes have passed, and by now the listeners are no longer impatient for an ending. They begin to await each new twist of the plot with pure surprise, even delight, having given up any idea of if and how the soldier will succeed, perhaps even having forgotten about the dragon and the princess. The mind is carefree and curious, taking pleasure in the creative and communal experience of the ongoing story within the present moment.

Storytelling engrosses us because the symbols and images, the narratives and landscapes, are present within our imagination. Hence the tale, although perhaps never heard before, is familiar. The experience feels natural and rich. Distraction is short-circuited as we settle into the satisfying invention of images arising in our own dreaming minds. Even the most restless adolescent discovers an effortless ability to focus. As listeners become more and more involved, a feeling akin to enchantment arises and the conceptual mind is gathered up into the story's ongoing events. An oasis amidst our everyday preoccupations, this refreshment can produce new insight or solutions, and is good practice in overcoming our need for busyness. However, just when we think that we have finally gotten somewhere, we discover another level of obstacle.

The soldier called out, but there was no answer. Again he was without hope, when he remembered the sword of might and called it from its sheath. The sword flew out and hacked the iron stones to dust. The soldier, on foot and alone, entered the dragon's cave.

The earth was rugged and unstable. Then he saw the glow of the princess's crown in the distance and hurried forward. Only then did he discover that he walked on the enormous body of the dragon and the head of the creature rested on the skirts of his beloved. The dragon roared, "You are no hero, but a fool to think that you can enter this cave and take away what is mine." For a moment the soldier was terrified, but after so many adventures he was not easily shaken and he called for the sword again. The sword flew from its sheath and sliced the dragon into a thousand pieces. The soldier huddled against the stone walls of the cave until the sword returned to his belt.

Then he turned to claim his bride. But there on a white stone, surrounded by the hacked-up dragon, lay the snake curled around itself seven times. The soldier sobbed, "I have worn you around my neck for seven years. I have traveled across the world, followed the witch, crossed an uncrossable ocean, and passed over an impassable mountain. I have made my way through an overgrown forest and stayed awake where heroes fall asleep. I have even killed a dragon. Every hero who kills a dragon marries a princess. What more must I do?"

We are all far too familiar with this scenario. Recently, in telling the story to a large audience of adults, there was a trickle of knowing laughter at this point in the story before a communal sigh of sympathy, and, finally, another deeper sigh as we adjusted ourselves to wait once more. There are ever more subtle levels of attachment to what we want both in the story and in life. And so the story goes on, taking us further, always true to the ways things really are. We are reminded that we will be tested again and again and will need a great deal of practice to overcome the deeply ingrained habits of our mind. The dragon may have been defeated, but, alas, the journey is not yet over. The tendency to impatience is strong but the story offers us a living template for perseverance, and the constant presence of the storyteller keeps us steady with warmth and an embodied voice.

> The snake said, "Soldier, you have killed. You must place me in the water of life and cleanse yourself." He asked, "And where can I find the water of life?" She answered, "Only Baba Yaga knows the way." And from behind the stones in the cave and the blood-drenched pieces of the dragon rose the mother of nature herself, the witch of all fairytales: Baba Yaga, the boney one. Laughing her stone-shattering laugh, she commanded, "Follow me," and she flew in her metal bowl from her brother's cave.

No doubt most of us have forgotten the story's beginning; now we are reminded that the soldier was returning from battle. Here, with him, we are shown that there are karmic debts or root causes to be cleansed, and that we had to discover patience, so that the hidden patterns or circumstances of our lives can be acknowledged.

> The snake slithered onto the soldier's neck again as he climbed on his horse and followed the witch. She took him to a clear blue lake in the middle of a forest. Not trusting her, he placed a branch in the water, and it burst into flame. In a fury, he yelled, "Take me to the water of life!" The witch took him to another forest where again he placed a dried branch in a lake only to see it crumble to dust. In a rage, he threatened, "If you don't take me to the water of life, I will kill you!" The Great Mother smiled and said, "If you kill me, who will take you to the water of life?"

Shantideva tells us that wholesome deeds amassed over a thousand eons will be destroyed in one moment of anger. The Great Mother is revealing to the soldier his own hidden well of anger, lack of trust, and ignorance. In this way it is neither suppressed nor ignored. This is her kindness. She gives him the chance to lay aside his arrogance, and our own arrogance is undone. We too remember that, regardless of the fact that he may have been a hired soldier fighting to survive, he has been engaged in killing and must be cleansed. On another level we are also instructed that listening together, there is no difference between ourselves and our neighbor—even an enemy can sit beside us and share the space with us as if we were at a feast. Everyone wants to find out what happens next. We are all tamed by such listening.

The soldier heard the words of the witch and stilled his heart. He asked humbly, "Old Mother, will you take me to the water of life?" She answered gently, "Since you asked, I will." Baba Yaga took him to a third forest where there was a lake bluer than the blue of the sky. He placed a branch in the water and watched as it flowered and bore fruit. The snake unwound from his neck and slid into the deep waters, as the witch vanished from sight.

But the princess did not return.

The soldier sat by the lake for a long time. At last, when he least expected it, the princess appeared. Together they climbed on his horse and rode to her parent's palace where they were wed. It is said that they sat on two thrones and ruled equally with wisdom and compassion for the benefit of everyone, and because of that everyone lived happily ever after.

Because we have become accustomed to waiting, the ending is neither victory nor solution—it is joy shared. We can experience a sense of "peaceful abiding." Within, where we have become the story, masculine and feminine have been joined. At the end of the story, returned again to our ordinary lives, we also feel connected to each other, patient, communicative. This is the great wedding, the shared meal among us, the great homecoming.

Once I told this tale to a group of three hundred second-graders who sat intent throughout. When we came to the end, a little girl seated in front of me took my hand and said, "I have forgotten the story already." I asked, "What happened?" She replied, "I got married." Whether or not we understood what she meant didn't matter. Everyone, including the teachers, the principal, and myself, laughed heartily because it also had happened to all of us.

THE HEN AND THE ROOSTER

continues...

THE youngest prince on the back of the three legged horse rode more slowly than he might have crawled, until he stopped near a meadow. There he wept. Not far from the prince was an old man, so bent over that his toes stepped on his beard. He was trying to water corn although no water fell from his pail. He heard the royal sobs and inquired, "Why are you weeping?" The prince felt the man's task was futile, but he told his story.

The old man lifted his head. "Don't think that your three-legged horse is useless," he said. "It alone can bring you to the young woman who has the rooster and hen that you seek." Staring at the horse, he said, "Tell that lame horse of yours, 'You are the best horse. I need your help badly!' It will take you across the sea to where the maiden can be found." And the prince continued his journey.

The revisioning of history is, therefore, also an act of prophecy - not prophecy in the sense of making predictions, for the universe is too free and open-ended for the manipulations of a religious egotism - but prophecy in the sense of seeing history in the light of myth.

WILLIAM IRWIN THOMPSON

T'Boli Dreaming

Keeping the Channels of a Culture Open

A NATIVE AMERICAN STORYTELLER in the Yukon suggested to an Icelandic novelist traveling to New York that she get in touch with me. We agreed to meet at a Greek diner on Broadway. Both writers and travelers interested in a similar process of creativity, we quickly became friends. I offered her my home while I traveled to the Philippines so she could finish her novel. In exchange, she read my coffee grinds, something my own Rumanian mother had done for me while I was growing up in Brooklyn.

Seated at my kitchen table, she upturned the drying coffee cup and asked me, "Is there something uncomfortable about this trip?"

"Yes," I answered, surprised. "I feel frightened of the week I am to spend with the T'Boli people in the south island of Mindanao. I know nothing about them."

"You will feel fear," she said, "and you will discover a treasure."

. . .

I arrived in Manila during monsoon season in early August. Manila is in Luzon, the northernmost island of the more than seven thousand islands awkwardly formed into a country by the colonial Spanish over three hundred years ago. Destroyed during World War II, Manila suffers the horrors of a modern-day city too quickly created in a third-world culture. There are no reminders of ancient history, and few traces of its colonial grace remain. What natural beauty it has to offer is hidden by pollution and overshadowed by dense poverty and overpopulation.

I was traveling to T'Boli, a territory of seven villages, as part of a month-long storytelling tour to gather stories. At that time my only encounter with T'Boli tribes had been the few paragraphs in *The Philippine Handbook*: "An estimated 200,000 T'Boli inhabit the Tiruray Highlands, a 2,000-square-km area within a triangle bounded by Surallah, Kiamba and Polomok..."

In Manila I found that any time I mentioned my upcoming visit to T'Boli I was greeted with tremendous interest, curiosity, and even awe. I was shown brass bells, beaded necklaces, photographs of elaborately costumed women, and treasured Tinaluk wall hangings, the sacred ceremonial cloth of the T'Boli.

Still, I felt a growing sense of unease. Why was I going to T'Boli? Was I to add to the increased exploitation by mining, forestry, and tourism? Worse, I knew nothing of their traditions or taboos. My coffee reading was of no consolation, although I reflected on it.

I have learned from my own travels and experiences that an outer journey is an inner journey. The most unexpected occurrences are usually the most significant, and the actual map is a secret map whose contours depend on my own receptivity to what unfolds moment to moment. I considered my journey to T'Boli a quest, a pilgrimage to a way of life rapidly vanishing from our planet.

In Manila, I said to myself, "It is best to surrender to the fact that I know nothing, and remain alert."

In fairytales, and esoteric and symbolic stories, it is the fool who becomes the hero or heroine. Sent out into the world, she does not know in which direction to travel. So she shoots an arrow, throws a stone or a feather. Where it lands is the direction in which she journeys.

I spent one week in Manila, hosted by the kindness and hospitality of the loveliest people in the world, surrounded by the shock of unending, miserable poverty and an unbreathable atmosphere. I looked forward to my trip south.

Upon my arrival in Davao on Mindanao, the southernmost island of the Philippines, an earthy, smiling woman greeted me at the airport. She placed a brass, black-beaded necklace around my neck, saying, "Welcome. The necklace is T'Boli."

The first evening in Davao, protected by an armed guard (wealthy families are often kidnapped by remnants of Marcos' rebel army), I was taken to dinner in the best Filipino restaurant. The other guests were a real estate mogul and executives from an auto company and an oil concern—men intent on bringing the Philippines "into the twenty-first century." The conversation revolved mainly around a golf tournament. No one inquired about my trip to T'Boli.

The next day our odd traveling crew began the journey: a translator from the tourist office, the driver of the air-conditioned white van, a T'Boli man returning to Lake Sebu after a market visit to sell Tinaluk in Davao, and me. "It is best to travel on Saturday," I was told. "You will be less conspicuous."

Davao is advertised as the largest city in the world, spreading out for miles and miles. With the added obstruction of traffic, stray chickens, and dogs, the trip was long. The urban landscape was a strange mix of palm trees, rickshaws, bustling markets, flamboyant flowers, and diesel buses packed with people. World War II jeeps painted in wild colors and splattered with Christian prayers mingled with vans carrying sad-faced pigs to the slaughter.

Suddenly, the city gave way to grassy hills, rice paddies, and boys riding on water buffaloes. The sunlight erased the memory of urban sprawl and we began to cheer up, until the smell of burning garbage hit our nostrils and a dark cloud of ash masked the road ahead. We rode through a modern nightmare of garbage dumps adorned with ash-dyed bamboo houses and thick-dust-covered children and cows. As my eyes adjusted, I was amazed at the ingenuity of these houses made of trash. The translator from the tourist office explained that these people make their living from sorting out the debris. I felt in awe of their resourcefulness.

Finally, we left the outskirts of the last large city behind, polluted and jumbled with every conceivable mode of transportation—sports cars, diesel buses, trucks, bicycle-drawn rickshaws, men on horseback, and farmers on caraboa. We rode in silence for hours bouncing over dirt roads deeply rutted from the rains.

When we came closer to South Cotabato the rains began. We stopped for lunch at an outdoor restaurant on Lake Sebu where the T'Boli live, and sat under a sideless thatched roof at the water's edge. The T'Boli catch fish in a banca (a carved-out tree trunk), cook them on an open fire, and serve them on a thick leaf. Skinny dogs lay under our table, where I proceeded to throw fragments of fish and bread, somewhat to the annoyance of my guide.

I looked out at the lake. Small hill-locked islands with bamboo houses dotted the water. Mountains in the distance. Smells of rain and forest.

An old woman at the back of a banca fished silently. Teenage boys paddling a flat boat took fish from her basket and brought them to the fire. Behind her were the patterned nets of new fisheries, a plan engineered by a European to increase the catch of fish from the lake. The birth of an industry. The sight of the nets sent chills down my spine; the driver had told me how quickly the ecological balance of the lake is shifting because of fisheries, mining, and forestry.

Humbled, I went to the T'Boli market. Crowded. Walking, shopping, clusters of people conversing. The foreignness and inaccessibility of the T'Boli seems startling. They stared at me momentarily, but had no interest in my presence. Only the sales-people seemed to take notice of me.

The T'Boli women in full traditional costume were stunning: small and Malaysian-looking in many-colored sarongs and deli-cately embroidered blouses; women and girls were adorned with foot-long earrings, layers of necklaces, hats as large as umbrellas, stacks of anklets and bracelets—red, blue, black, white, green, turquoise. I had no reference point for these faces born out of a 25,000-year-old history of trading between Indonesia, these islands, China, Africa, Polynesia, and Arabia. The words of a Maori chant came to mind: *The power and the prestige, the garments of your ancestors.*

There was a stirring of interest in me over the next two days, as it became known that I was a storyteller. I had attended a T'Boli wedding. I was seen walking around, taking a trip in a boat on the lake. People offered to tell me stories, and a dance concert was arranged in the lower room of the T'Boli guide's family's bamboo house. Women performed in full costume one at a time (including a beautiful swallow dance, as graceful as the most elegant Javanese court dance), accompanying themselves with drums and gongs made from parts of trees, rubber shoes, and kitchen pots. While, in the background, a row of old men watched a television show featuring the new Spanish Miss Amer-ica dancing flamenco-style.

But where were the stories? At last I was granted an interview with a princess who was a weaver. My translator was Peter Corado, a T'Boli lawyer. I hoped to find a story about the origin of weaving. I know many myths from Africa and Polynesia about weaving and the origin of language, and the traditional Tinaluk fabric of the T'Boli was fascinating to me.

> The ceremonial clothing of both men and women,
> Tinaluk is a deep brown abraca cloth tie-dyed with
> intricate red and beige designs. Natural vegetable dyes
> are used to stain the fibers before the cloth is woven.

> The cloth has great significance for the T'Boli. It's one
> of the traditional properties exchanged at the time of
> marriage and is used as a covering during birth to
> ensure a safe delivery. The T'Boli believe that cutting
> the cloth will cause serious illness or death. If it is sold,
> a brass ring is often attached to appease the spirits.[7]

A stalk of notched bamboo served as a ladder to the house
of Princess Diwa Tel, alias Ye Wala. I took off my sandals and
climbed up behind Peter. The floor was made of thin strips of
bamboo, and through the spaces I saw the earth far below. Unable
to conceive of walking on what looked like paper, I froze. Peter
pulled me in. I felt as though I were standing on the thread of
a hammock.

The old woman was seated by an opening in the wall which
served as a window. She said, "I am sick and cannot speak for a
long time." I inquired quickly about the story of the first weavings.
In the center of the room I saw her loom, a half-woven Tinaluk
growing from its base. In baskets next to the loom were balls of
tie-dyed fibers made of banana hemp.

She explained in detail how the Tinaluk is made—the plants
chosen, bark stripped, boiled, and prepared, dyed, blessed, and
so on. She then told how each single pattern is dreamed by the
weaver. "Each design is new. No other person has made this
exact design. They come in dreams in three ways: from the ancestors, from one's mother, and from one's own dream. The channel
of the dream must be open." To be woven, each new pattern
must be dreamed anew.

"I never watch television or listen to the radio," she said.
"There is an evil spirit in the television." The channel would be
disturbed, clogged. Then the dreaming would not happen.

The blouses that the T'Boli women wear are famous for their
intricacy and uniqueness. They are red and black and white, the
colors of the alchemy of the soul in fairytales. "Some blouses
take one month to finish. Some—the ones embroidered with

small seashells—can take one or two years to complete." Again and again she emphasized the importance of listening to the ancestors by keeping open the place to dream.

I was very moved as she spoke. Having seen the fisheries and the manufactured batik-like fabrics in the market the day before, I said, "The world is changing all around you. It is inevitable. Someone will come and convince the T'Boli to have their patterns manufactured to make money. What must remain for the people to still be T'Boli?"

She answered in the pleasing rhythmic pattern of T'Boli language. Her words were couched in the incessant hum and trill of birds and crickets from the rain forest that surrounded the house. As she spoke, I became aware of a new sound: the overwhelming metallic drone of a motorcycle which was being repaired down the road. I leaned forward to hear her words and Peter's translation.

"Women must continue to weave, to make jewelry, baskets, to sing and tell stories," she stated. Her daughter brought out her tribal clothing: necklaces, bracelets, earrings, the thirteen-pound brass belt adorned with T'Boli bells and carved metal, an embroidered shirt, eight thick brass anklets and six wrist bracelets, the beaded wooden hairpiece, and a pair of earrings which extended from the earlobe and wrapped around the neck like a collar.

She put them on with her daughter's help. Transforming herself into a veritable temple deity, she became a visible map of her ancestors, her culture, and nature. She smiled proudly. Then she lifted her skirt and showed her tattooed calves, which would make her recognizable at death to the ancestors in the other world.

Again, the words of a Maori chant returned to me: *The womb of the earth is your pillow.*

"And what if these things are washed away by flood, or earthquake, or are mass manufactured for sale without dreaming?" I asked. "It may happen. What must be left for T'Boli to exist?"

Now she grew quiet. She nodded. Peter, a man educated in the West, listened intently. I looked out at the forest and the houses. A horse, fleeing, suddenly dashed from behind another bamboo house. Three men chased it. The caraboa tied by its nose to a log looked unconcerned. The trees moved. I felt the bamboo floor sway in a sensuous response to the wind. I waited.

When she answered, she spoke confidently, looking into my eyes directly for the first time. I answered her with my own eyes as Peter translated. She said, "Sharing. Hospitality." On cue, the sound of the motorcycle engine stopped.

Her daughters served us coffee as she described the necessity of living together, of sharing all one has with others, whether family or strangers. Time seemed to stretch.

The princess moved uncomfortably. I recalled the warning about her poor health at the outset of our meeting and began to thank her—for her time, for her generosity, for her profound teaching. We offered gifts of rice, liquor, beads, and money. Her reception of them was simple. She held them, acknowledged them, and placed them beside a basket on the floor.

As we climbed down the ladder, I saw an exquisite old basket near the loom. She called out to Peter, "It is an old one. Made by a Mindaya (another neighboring tribe) woman. I traded for it in the market a long time ago."

She looked fragile, her house so flimsy.

Our eyes met again, a simple human connection, not extraordinary or special, and a light went on in my mind. The subtlety and meaning of what she had just said struck me: "Sharing. Hospitality."

The drive back from T'Boli to Davao was more harrowing and twice as long. Several hours into the trip the car broke down. While it was being repaired, we waited more than four hours inside an airless fast-food restaurant in a new mall.

When we finally arrived in the city and climbed out of the van, our T'Boli guide opened his tattered suitcase and gave me a gift—a hand-dyed Tinaluk with a frog and seed pattern. Nothing that I had to offer to him or to Peter or the princess could be half as valuable...except perhaps my gratitude and respect as I write this.

Four days after my visit to the T'Boli, a volcano on one of the lakes that had been quiet for hundreds of year erupted, destroying people, hundreds of houses, T'Boli artifacts, and animals.

What did I learn from my journey to this remote Filipino village? That the forms of culture—stories, houses, clothing, carvings, weavings, songs, dances, tattoos—are the visible means of protecting knowledge, without which we would be less than human. They are a visible map to an invisible world within us, a map that leads to no place and every place. Moreover, that if we can remember the ways to sink into reciprocal being, if the channel is left open to dreaming from that country within each one of us, we can dream all that is needed into being again.

This is the treasure I brought back with me from T'Boli.

Tsatayeva tells us that a fairytale that doesn't frighten is not a fairytale. It is a terror that transports us to a place where Dostoyevsky was transported when he was condemned to death, this most precious place, the most alive, where you tell yourself you are going to receive the axe's blow, and when you discover, by the axe's light, what Kafka made Moses say: "How beautiful the world is even in its ugliness." It's at this very moment, as Blanchot would say, that "We see the light."

—HELENE CIXOUS, *Three Steps on the Ladder of Writing*

Through the Story's Terror

*F*EAR IS THE UNCOMPROMISING compassion of the hero and heroine in story, as well as in life. She shakes loose the walls of our fixed ideas and conceptions, waking us up trembling and alert, to experience the reality of our inner world and the invisible realm of spirit and ancestors that lay locked behind thick chains of conventional logic. Fear is not to be avoided, repressed, or conquered, for from the very depths of fear arise fearlessness, awareness, and wisdom. The acknowledgment and experience of fear is the door that opens us to heightened presence and perception through which we learn to live in the world as it is.

The experience of fear is physical. It is neither imaginary nor conceptual, but is known directly through the body. Thus, one of the ways in which traditional people have prepared their children to live in the world, to learn and survive, has been through the live telling of myth, legend, fairytale, and true story.

The experience of events is known through an actual psychic enactment: the fear is confronted and endured in the imagined story as a kind of practice, process, or ritual. When Frances Harwood, anthropologist, asked a Sioux elder why people tell stories, he answered, "In order to become human beings." She asked, "Aren't we all human beings already?" He smiled. "Not everyone makes it."

The most powerful stories, those that are told with knowledge and experience informing the storyteller, are capable of engendering a visceral, imaginative, psychological, and intuitive response during the telling. Of all the stories that pierce to the heart of fear, the fairytales succeed best, second only to retellings of long-unspoken personal narratives born of crisis or bliss. The direct involvement in becoming the story makes it an experience, one that occurs at the moment of the telling. A story is not an explanation. It is lived between teller and listener; it resonates far beyond the content. The text alone, separated from the enlivening experience, can be analyzed, but the result is different. It is not a transformative event. In other words, genuine story manifests as it is heard, when the listener is drawn out of self-consciousness—the thinking mind held entranced by the ongoing logic of the narrative—and becomes everything in the story. The meaning and the power of the story do not reside in the content alone; rather, they unfold in the dynamic process of listening/creating.

The storytelling is potent because it is a physical experience. The whole person is engaged in the making of meaning and story. Mind, body, and heart are synchronized and activated. The embodied listener is alert, with senses heightened, and naturally creates image and meaning from association, feeling, memory, dream, and a ceaseless source of archetypal symbol within. It is the holistic activity of listening, not the conceptual content of the text or plot alone, where true learning takes place. During the event, the inherent and natural wisdom of ear, eye, and heart are given voice.

In the Turkish fairytale of "The Three Golden Apples," the

youngest prince, the most fearful of the three, is the one who kills the monster that has caused massive hunger in the world. When the monster is dead, the audience cheers, relieved, breathing heavily, having overcome the monster and their own fear that they could not slay it. Then, just as the prince is about to return home, he is betrayed by his brothers and has to confront an even more challenging situation.

***

An old man advised him, "I know the only way back home. You must walk into this meadow and close your eyes. You will hear three three-legged horses running. Jump on one, keeping your eyes closed. If it is the white one, you will return. If it is the red, you will remain here. If it is the black one, you will descend into another world beneath this one."

The trembling prince leaps, eyes closed, onto the black horse. He descends to a desolate world ruled by a flesh-eating dragon that is ultimately responsible for the drought that had produced the original monster.

This kind of storytelling, story, and listening is akin to traditional rites of passage that create the ground for something to happen, for the practitioner to pass through a threshold of fear to know the self and to face the awesome sacredness of life. The feeling of communion, relaxation, enchantment, and refreshment that is felt during and after a storytelling is proof that this has occurred. Something has opened, widened inside the listener, that makes visible the invisible world of image. "I didn't see you when you told the story," remarked a fourth-grade girl. I asked, "What did you see?" "My story," she answered.

It is like dreaming wide awake. Although the narrative plot carried the logical mind along, entranced with curiosity to know what will happen next, the images and meaning of story sink downward, plunging the listener deeper and deeper, drawing upward the richest source of intuitive knowing, memory, compassion, and wisdom. It is a gossamer, yet vivid, multilayered shadow play, which cannot be reconstructed by the logical mind.

It is dreaming. It is awake. It is alert.

. . .

Louis Bird, an Omushkego Cree elder, said about telling stories:

> How do you train your young ones or your next generation so they survive? To have skills you need a lot of education first. You need to see and act and experience everything but you must learn before you acquire skills to survive. The lessons are hard in the beginning. The lessons as story are told as soon as they can understand. They are geared as they grow. They change. There are different ways of telling them as the person grows older. They are flexible. They work because they also make the mind of the person flexible, able to live that kind of life. These stories help you live.

Life is dangerous without skills. The inner person has to be prepared to sustain the unpredictability of weather and mind, the intensity of experiencing sorrow and joy, acknowledging fear, change, and the touch of death. Without passing through the pulsating threshold of fear, the hero or heroine would remain ever stuck at the beginning of the story, enclosed in a fortress of systems and rigid beliefs.

In the Native American Modoc myth of Kokolimalayas (the Bone Man), an orphaned boy, Nulwee, is told that he must kill the monster that murdered his parents, destroyed his village, and caused the earth to be barren. His grandmother tells him the story. He is terrified. "How can I kill that monster?" The listener, hearing the story, asks the same thing. The boy's preparation is long and surprising. He is warned against waking the monster, but disobeys. He wakes the monster, watching him grow bone by bone back to life. He feeds the Bone Man, providing him with strength and size. Only then does he confess to his grandmother what he has inadvertently done. She then prepares him for the next stage of his initiation, more fearful than the first. He must learn how to use the bow and arrow skillfully to save his life, and to think clearly on his feet while knowing absolute fear.

"Grandma," stutters the boy dressed for battle, "I am afraid."

She answers, while pushing him out the door to what might be his death, "A good warrior is always afraid."

In this way, the boy is educated to overcome his fear, not by escaping it, but by a total conscious immersion in it. It is as if hidden in the darkest recesses of our fear lies the sustaining awareness of fearlessness. We, the listener, tremble for the boy Nulwee, because we have seen the monster, and we tremble for ourselves, who will now confront him again.

The secret of the power of story is the essential realization that what happens to the character in the story is not important. What is of value is what happens to we who listen. In truth, the character does not exist except in our own invention of him or her. We have manifested all the characters—even the landscape— from within, just as a disciple embodies the energy of a deity within themselves during practice and prayer, or the masked dancer calls for the spirits of the gods and demons and brings them to our world to be seen, felt, feared, and loved.

Of course, the listener is tricked, just as the boy is tricked. The necessary activity is to awaken the monster in the story and in ourselves. Logically, none of us would do it. In the fairytale the heroine is warned, "Don't open that door," or "You can use any key but the tiny silver one. Don't use that key." Or, as Nulwee's grandmother cautions, "Sing the old holy songs and not your childish songs." Frightened into forgetfulness, Nulwee sings those childish songs, bringing the skeleton back to life. Fear numbs the logical mind, awakening the dreaming mind to carry out what needs to be done.

The listener hears the warning and undergoes the consequences simultaneously. It is we who invest the monster with being, dress him into reality, and raise him up bone by bone. We feed him while the grandmother we have conjured waits in the distance, and the ghost of invoked ancestors watch. We even summon the barren land and silent sky, pregnant with possibility and ready to be renourished.

Such profuse and brilliant creativity sleeps within, on the other side. It is fear that crumbles the thick walls of familiar convention and habitual patterns of ignorance. And it is fear that opens us to what treasures lie in wait within. In fairytales it is so often the youngest, least developed of the characters who is able to break through convention and acknowledge fear with humility and compassion. The trembling hero of "The Golden Apples" faces more and more fearful obstacles until he gives up hope. He destroys the final and most gruesome monster without hesitation to save twelve eagle babies in an uncanny place, two worlds beneath our own. In gratitude, the eagle mother attempts to save him and carry him home on her back. Midway, she loses strength and they begin to plummet toward death. The hero has no more fear of death. It has been transformed into compassion, which arises simply as a selfless act:

The prince felt pity for the mother eagle and her children. He took out a tiny knife and cut flesh from his own leg to feed her. When she tasted human flesh, she did not swallow, but she was nourished by his kindness and carried him back to this world.

Her flight, like the shaman's flight, carries us back home. With her magic she healed him and then flew back to her children.

And so the young warrior Nulwee, instructed by his grandmother, confronts the monster for the last time, knowing full well that not only is his own life at risk but also those of his grandmother, the people of the future, and the earth.

In the fairytale, the hero still has to outwit his evil brothers to win the princess and to tell his story from beginning to end.

> The boy's heart beat swiftly. His entire body shook, but he pressed his feet
> to the earth and faced the monster. His arrow pierced the monster and the
> Bone Man's heart flew from him. Nulwee caught it in his basket and began
> to run. The monster stumbled after him, but without a heart, the Bone Man
> had no strength and fell to the ground.

In the myth, Nulwee throws the monster's heart into the sky
and it transforms into thunder, bringing the long-needed rain.

At the threshold of the new or unknown is fear. The knowledge
of fear is not abstract; instead, it is central to our awakening. In
the cremation grounds in India, the Hindu pilgrim invokes the
wrathful aspect of Shiva: "The world considers you inauspicious,
O Destroyer of Fear, who plays in the Smashan smeared with
the ashes from funeral pyres, wearing a necklace of human skulls,
with ghouls for comrades. But for those who remember You
with devotion, O Bestower of Boons, You are supremely
auspicious."

Ultimately, fear is in service of compassion. We, who have
become all the characters, feel the pain and selflessness of the
prince who offers his own flesh. The feeling evoked by this
fearless act arises forcefully because we have been opened and
prepared by the deep listening. Furthermore, because we are
everyone, not hero or heroine alone, the consequences of actions
have been enacted and felt within us. Such unbiased awareness
is the mother of true compassion.

The terrible demons, wrathful goddesses and gods, monsters
and nightmares, are hideous to the naked eye. "How frightening
she is," we remark on seeing the eight-headed Mahakalis depicted
in temples, or the headless blood-drinking goddesses of India
and Tibet, or the unbearable monsters in our own dreams. Robert
Svoboda, writing about the cremation ground rites, expounds:
"Most people, unfortunately, are so attached to their snares [the
emotions which cloud the mind] that they shrink from her in
fear...thinking, 'She wants to kill me.' She does want to kill you—
the false you, the limited you, which is accrued over so many
births—when she cuts off your head, your mind becomes firm,

unwavering in its concentration, which enables you to succeed."

Recently, I was barred from telling ghost stories to children in a conservative school, because of the school's religious beliefs and because it would frighten them. The level of child and adult violence in this city was astonishing. Later that afternoon, in another school, after an hour of stories, the children asked for more. "What shall I tell?" I asked. In unison they called out, "Something scary." And so I proceeded, slowly, deliciously, to bring ghosts and demons into view, in the visceral, vivid, yet safe world of story—knowing that if I did not, the demons would clamor for attention and rise up again and again in our world. In this world, we do not know what to do with them except to build more prisons in which to control and hide them, or to make more wars to conquer them. The fairytale offers us a daring solution within ourselves.

When the two deceptive brothers of the prince see him, they say, "Don't believe a word he says. He is a liar and a coward." However, when the prince tells his story, those who hear him know it is the truth, and the two older brothers are placed in a dungeon. The prince marries the youngest princess, whom he brought back to this world, but the golden apples don't grow again.

Not until the princess becomes queen and the prince becomes king. Then, united, they visit the two brothers, who by now have understood the full consequences of their evil. They who feared fear and caused betrayal become the protectors of the kingdom and vow to serve the king and queen and all the people, even the animals.

And that winter the three golden apples grew on the tree. There was no hunger of heart or belly, and everyone lived happily ever after. Those of you who have listened and made the golden apples grow in your minds, may you live as well.

THE HEN AND THE ROOSTER

continues...

THE old man gave the youngest prince more instructions: "The maiden with the birds is seated on a cloud. If she sees you, she will turn you to dust and wind. When you arrive, you must hide. But all is not lost. When she lies down to sleep, she unbinds her hair and hangs it from the sky to the earth. Twist her hair around your arm and hold tight even when she wakes and screams, 'Unbind my hair. I am burning.' Hearing those words, take a firmer hold. She will beg you to release her hair, making the promise, 'I swear to give you the earth, the sky, the sea, and the whole world.' Don't believe her!"

The prince listened. "Only when she swears by the rooster and the hen that she will give you, will she follow as your wife. Then you should let free your grip." The prince agreed.

"I forgot something," the old man added. "Be careful of the bald-headed lute player on the cloud beneath hers. He would also like to carry her and her birds away. However, he has not received these instructions. When she swears by the birds, whisk her away without hesitation."

The prince thanked the old man. He said to his three-legged horse, "Beautiful horse, I need you." Immediately, the horse flew into the sky as fast as the wind. It soared over earth and sea to another land and brought the prince to the place where the maiden with the birds and the long hair of gold was living.

I remember the lamplighter. It was just when the sun was setting and the colors of the houses were dim that he came down the street carrying a long pole which encased a light. He would open the glass door on the streetlamp, move a lever and ignite the gas. At first, the lamp glowed like a tiny moon. Then the magic began. Everything became brilliant on the street. It was like a fairyland. I always waited for the lamplighter in the evening. He made light dawn in the middle of increasing dark. It was splendid.

—FLORENCE ALTERMAN, The Lamplighter[8]

The Lamplighter

The Storyteller in the Modern World

$\mathcal{S}$ EVERAL YEARS AGO I opened the door to a classroom and saw two boys fighting. The teacher was enraged and the children were either frozen at their desks or shoving each other. The air was thick with anger. "Who are you?" the teacher asked. "I'm the storyteller," I replied, feeling like a doctor arriving in an emergency room. I slowly walked to the front of the room and said, "I came to tell you a story." Even the fighters took their seats. After a moment, the fidgeting settled and all eyes opened wide with expectation.

"Once upon a time there was a group of girls who were jealous of one girl, for she had a necklace more beautiful than theirs."[9] Slowly, slowly, we entered the world of the story. The teacher sat down to listen. "In this village, a necklace was a sign of one's womanhood and one's power. The jealous girls plotted against the beautiful girl. They dug holes by the riverside and hid their necklaces; then they called to the girl saying, 'The river god is going to cause a flood. Everyone in the village will die. If you throw your necklace into the river, just as we have thrown ours, no one will die.'"

Gradually, the air in the room changed. All the anger dissolved as confused emotions went to work in sympathy for the mistreated girl. I could feel the children's measured, even breathing as the story's events unfolded. At first, only their eyes glowed, but with the growing intensity of their feelings and imaginings, the color returned to their cheeks.

"The girl was kind. She threw her necklace into the water." As my hands mirrored the necklace falling into the river and the rhythm of my voice echoed the inevitability of the events soon to follow, the bond between the children and me was complete. We relaxed into the rhythm of the words. We relaxed into our mutual visualization.

An irresistible familiarity urges us into a story. I have had this experience in many different situations, including audiences of sophisticated theater-goers, family groups, elderly people, foreign diplomats, even a group of men on a New York street. And always, the spell of the storyteller's story overcame whatever obstacles existed in the environment, causing the audience to fall into the story, just as the children did in this classroom.

Over and over again, when a story ends, I have sat in silence with my audience, relishing for a moment longer the delightful experience of renewal. We are inspired by the excitement of sharing our lives in the moment, in sharing the tenderness of our frailties as human beings. It is as if gray clouds have cleared, and the sun is shining.

Today the storyteller is like a lamplighter: one who ignites our imaginations—awakens dormant feelings within us, sparks the very heart of our humanity—illuminating us from within. A story told reaches beyond the boundaries of history, ethnicity, literature, or religion. It moves us beyond our personal prejudices and associations. It kindles the embers of our basic human goodness.

We have lost touch with the time when an entire village hung on story; when every aspect of life was presented, questioned, and given meaning by story, music, dance, art, architecture, and metaphor. But we still possess that common bond of existence whose continuous story we share with everyone. This is the source and power of the revival in storytelling today. The renaissance of oral tradition fills a basic need; it is as nourishing as good food.

Social scientists, paleontologists, and physicists investigating the nature of the human mind, patterns of cultural behavior, and world literature, continually return to a discussion of story.[10] Their research reveals that for a culture to be healthy there must be the communication of story.

Laurens van der Post writes:

> The story was his [the Bushman's] most sacred possession. These people knew what we do not: that without a story you have not got a nation, or culture, or a civilization. Without a story of your own to live, you haven't got a life of your own...I feel that we today, who are in a period of transition of extreme peril, by taking in these images and stories, by swilling them around in our mind, can honor them in ourselves too. By taking these patterns of renewal [stories] to the place in ourselves where there is water, and where reeds and flowers grow, we can stimulate our own awareness. There is in all of us an immense Stone Age activity, a mythological activity, to which we do not attach nearly enough importance.[11]

Paleontologist Richard Leakey suggests that storytelling organized human society.[12] Storytelling was an important activity for early peoples. Since the human mind is the most unpredictable element of life, the narrating of stories drew people together and organized them through their sharing of perceptions.

It is important to remember that storytelling, as we know it today, is different from oral traditions of the past. In many cases, a spoken myth was incorporated as part of a ceremony or implicit in sculpture or dance. Often, a story was merely alluded to, not told from beginning to end, because everyone knew the tale or would come to know it over a lifetime.

In our society, we lack shared stories; we have no common spiritual and social rituals where people gather to connect with their basic humanity, their link with common ancestors and the fact of death, and social concerns for the benefit of themselves, each other, and the world.

The storyteller can play a significant role. Whether a telling is a sacred story incanted as part of a ceremony, an epic told in the courts of kings and queens, a performance at a storytelling festival, or a family incident whispered at a child's bedside, it is a ritual.

Ritual is a formal and repeated event that leads people through a psychological or spiritual transformation so they are inwardly refreshed and reconnected to their ancestors, themselves, their society, and the world. Ritual can also be explained as an activity that evokes the sacred, or that which is beyond itself. Ritual confirms our deepest human values: the presence of shared mystery; the magic of language; a knowledge of opinions; inspiration for growth; awareness of death and the continuity of life.

It is incredible to realize that a storyteller can stand, using a microphone, before a thousand people, and have the same depth of response as when he or she sits with a small, intimate group.

Like all rituals, storytelling has form: an invocation or entrance, a beginning, a middle, and an end. The ritual has already begun as soon as the storyteller walks onto the stage. Everyone's attention is focused. This is akin to the lights dimming in a theater, or the vocal ululations or ringing of bells that sometimes mark the beginning of an event and work to transform the space.

The beginning of the story itself creates an imaginative land-scape through which we will travel. It also draws the listener into direct relationship with the storyteller. This reciprocity ensures that the listeners are participants, rather than observers. It is a dance where instead of dancers holding hands, minds link in a reverie of silent images. Because of this reciprocity, the ritual can occur.

It is ultimately the performer's responsibility to invite this unique relationship. If the teller merely "enacts" the story, or repeats it verbatim without conviction or compassion, a transformation never takes place—only the words are heard.

. . .

Let us go back to our story.

The beautiful girl threw her necklace into the river. Then the jealous girls dug up their own necklaces, put them back on, and returned to the village, laughing. The beautiful girl began to cry. Then she decided to dive into the river and get back her necklace.

Storytelling is a living art that takes place in the present between people. It is not a solo performance. The narrative urges the listener out of self-consciousness and into the story. As the imaginative response becomes more and more vivid, the listeners participate in a heightened awareness of the event, as in ritual.

This absorption instigates a calm and dignified state where mind and body synchronize. As a young man once said to me, "When I listen to stories, I feel massaged through my whole body." We are being prepared to experience the mystery.

She didn't know what was in the river. She didn't know how deep the water was. But she dove into the river.

The voice of the storyteller, like a melody, provokes a depth of hearing which allows for feeling and imaging beyond the meaning of the words themselves. We see/hear/feel the laughter, the crying, and the dive into the water. As a story is told, there is no time to reflect on a single detail or turn back a page. The story moves forward like the river itself and we must follow to discover what happens next.

Slowly, she sank to the bottom of the river. There sat a hideous old woman, naked and covered with her own hair. And on her face and body were open sores. "What are you doing here?" she asked. Trembling, the girl answered, "I came for my necklace."

Engaged in the momentum of the ritual, every gesture or sound becomes potent. Through a change in voice, a variation in pacing, and the evocation of the character through a single gesture, the images shimmer between listeners and teller. It is like entering the many rooms inside of rooms in a Persian miniature, or viewing layers of transparent scenery superimposed upon each other in a shadow play.

So much depends on the presence of the storyteller, embodied and available, and their knowledge of the way in which story functions into the response of audience. This knowing informs the voice with warmth, clarity, emotion and a beckoning of listener to respond because it is their story now as well.

The old woman said, "If you want your necklace, lick clean my sores." The beautiful girl licked clean the old woman's sores. In return, the old woman protected her from a terrible people-eating demon.

The meaning of the story within the telling has a profound psychological effect. The listener undergoes the story. At the bottom of the river each person meets his or her own demon and beautiful girl. Thus as guide and friend, the storyteller is a lamplighter who illuminates and reveals the details of our own imagination. The actual journey remains personal, while the public quality of the event acknowledges that we are not alone.

In the past, people came to the storyteller with questions. Today, the storyteller reminds people that there *are* questions. This is an important job—to tell the right story at the right moment.

I know the stories that I tell are powerful, but I do not fully understand their meaning. Each one holds a secret. The mystery remains in the story. For the mystery to manifest, the story has to be told. Then, the mystery lives. It emerges between me and my listeners in the telling.

. . .

When people censor a story—removing or diluting what appears to be dangerous or unpleasant—in an effort to protect the listener (child or adult), the potency of the story is lost. The listener is actually in greater danger.

In story, these so-called "evil" characters and situations play out their dramas with full energy and consequence, and in so doing, they are acknowledged and resolved by listeners in the safe and special process of oral tradition. If the demonic and the fearful are ignored, we will not be prepared. Their destructive power will be felt in our everyday activities. As we discover in many stories, *if* it is acknowledged, even when it is feared, it is transformed or it rewards us greatly.

> Then the old woman gave the beautiful girl a necklace even more beautiful than the one she had lost.

In traditional cultures, ritual and story provided a means of understanding the witches and demons. Lacking a singular mythology that presents a method of befriending our fears, we in the Western cultures are rediscovering the ancient uses of storytelling.

The essential reward of the telling is enchantment. Enchantment is defined as "a state of being under a spell," or "a state of being highly delighted." The derivation of the word is from the Latin *cantare*, to sing. The prefix "en" means "wrap up in," or "make into." Being under the spell of the storyteller's words creates a state of being wrapped in a song, or in-chanted. We are enchanted by the storyteller's voice, the meaning of the words, the rhythm of the story and our own imaginations.

It is then that we feel, beneath the content of each story, another story as old and as fresh as time itself, which we share with every living thing.

The experience of such involvement is a state of being highly delighted. Delight is defined as "deep gratification." "De" means "from," and "light" is said to be "the essential condition of vision," or "mental and spiritual enlightenment."

The old woman told the girl to go back to her village and live just as before. "But as you walk down the road," she said, "you'll find a smooth, round stone. Pick it up and throw it into the river." And the girl did just what the old woman told her.

In each story, as in each ritual, the content and the form is instruction. It is ultimately up to each participant to discern those instructions and follow them, to find or not find the stone and return it or not return it to the river.

When the jealous girls saw the new necklace they grew curious. "Where did you find it?" they asked, feigning friendship. The girl told them about the old woman at the bottom of the river. They didn't even wait for the end of the story. They ran to the river and dove in. But when the old woman bade them lick clean her sores, they refused. "We just came for necklaces," they said, disgusted. The demon appeared and ate those girls all up. And that was that.

....

With the words "and that was that," the story is ended. The ritual is complete. The audience is returned to their ordinary world. It is now their story.

Before a performance the storyteller's responsibility is to themselves and the preparation of story. But during a performance the responsibility is to the listener. The storyteller brings the story to life to evoke the listener's own story, and the teller is acutely aware of the audience's response.

Storytelling is a form of *entertainment*. The root definition is provocative and dynamic *entre*, the French for "between," and *tennis*, to hold—to hold between. It is also defined as "to receive and to provide for," and "to distract." But it is a very special distraction designed to enchant and delight. It has the effect of putting people more directly in relationship to themselves. Perhaps we could define entertainment as "enter attainment."

Just as the girl returned to her village with a treasure, the listener returns to his or her own life with a gift.

When a lamp is lit, it first glows from within. But as it bursts into flames, it illuminates beyond itself to others.[13]

Today, such participation in story is precious and powerful.[14]

Once, after I told "The Necklace" in a high school auditorium, a teacher was astonished at the rapt attention of the students. She said to me, "They want to hear more stories. I think they are looking for their own story. They feel disconnected from themselves. Perhaps the storytelling gives them a way of organizing their search."

In telling stories we nourish ourselves and our world. We make light dawn in the middle of increasing darkness. It is splendid.[15]

How would it be if in the dark of the month,
with no moon, I were to enter the most strange and
frightening places, near tombs and in the thick of
the forest, that I might come to understand fear and
terror. And doing so, a wild animal would approach
or the wind rustle the leaves and I would think,
"perhaps the fear and terror, now comes."

And being resolved to dispel the hold of that fear
and terror, I remained in whatever posture arose,
sitting or standing, walking or lying down. I did
not change until I had faced that fear and terror in
that very posture, until I was free of its hold upon
me. And having this thought, I did so. By facing
the fear and terror I became free.

—THE BUDDHA SHAKYAMUNI

Evil in the World

A *Discourse on a Hassidic Tale*

Two years ago I had a surprise phone call from Monsieur Jean Sviadac, a friend and storytelling mentor who was visiting New York from Paris. We had first met at the Musee de L'Homme at an international conference in 1989. During our first conversation he told me a Hassidic story about death. I had just learned that I had cancer and was facing the possibility of my own death. The story quenched my need at the time for faith. Jean did not know this at the time. About his storytelling he said, "I am not a performer. I only tell a tale if I feel it will benefit." It did. He tells Hassidic tales, and Sufi stories like those of Hodja Nasruddin. "These tales are a sudden shock which wakes up a deeper awareness in the listener." Each time we met, he told me the story that I needed to hear.

At this latest meeting, he said, "I just thought of a tale that I read over thirty years ago. I have not thought of it until today. I will tell it to you." Since the story was an oral and vivid telling, and I was deeply moved, I will recount it as I have recalled it and retold it since:

....

The child of village Jews was not interested in the study of Torah. He was a wild boy, driven by curiosity. His natural wisdom was beyond his age. Sitting in the cheder, school room, was impossible for him. The hope of his parents was that one day he would outgrow his boundless energy and bend his mind to study. However, after an afternoon of play with Hassidic children, the boy returned home weeping. "Please, the children have told me about a Tzaddik, a holy man, in the next village. I must visit the Tzaddik."

The ordinary man and his wife saw the Hassidim as madmen, ecstatics, and the Tzaddik as a dangerous imposter. "I refuse to take you to the Tzaddik," stated the father. Filled with longing, the child begged until his parents agreed. Dismayed, the mother warned, "If there is any sign or ill omen on the journey you must return home immediately."

The boy and his father did not go far from their village when a wheel fell off the carriage. "It is an evil omen," said the father and returned home. The boy's sorrow could not be quelled. He begged incessantly, "My life depends on my meeting the Tzaddik." His mother and father responded angrily, "The man is neither holy nor wise, but undisciplined and unreasoning. Forget this strange request." However, the child's desire to see the Tzaddik increased every day until his eyes dried from too much crying.

Again, the mother and father, who loved their son, agreed to take him. And again, the mother warned, "If there is a single omen against this journey, bring my son home immediately." They set out again. This time there was no difficulty.

They arrived in the village of the Tzaddik and went to an inn. No sooner did they sit down to eat and drink, than a man entered the inn and sat down beside them. "What is your business?" inquired the stranger.

"My son demands to see the Tzaddik in this village," answered the father.

The stranger's eyes widened. He stood up, throwing his hands in the air. "The man is insane. He is a raving lunatic and not a holy person. You cannot take this child to see him. The child will be in danger."

Thanking the stranger for his good advice, the father returned home.

"That was more omen than I needed to know that everything we have heard about the Tzaddik is correct. There will be no more talk of such foolishness. Tomorrow you must go to study, to study."

The little boy sat silent as they rode home. He lay down on his bed upon return. But he did not go to cheder the next day or the next. He refused to eat. He did not speak except once to beg his parents to take him to the Tzaddik. Stubbornly, the father said, "He will recover. Let him lie in his bed until he is ready to study the Torah." However, he did not regain his strength and within weeks the little boy died.

The father and mother knew unceasing anguish and guilt. The father set out to find the Tzaddik and ask why their son had died. He arrived at night at the same inn. The same stranger entered the inn and sat down beside him. "My friend, you are very sad. Where is your child, the beautiful child that desired to see the Tzaddik?"

"My son died a few days ago and I have come to see the Tzaddik," answered the man sorrowfully.

This time the stranger threw back his head and laughed victoriously. "I am Satan," he said. "Your son was a holy child. And if he had met the Tzaddik, the light coming forth from both of their hearts would have joined and risen to heaven, illuminating this world, leaving no place for my evil."

Listening

When I heard the story I was stunned. At that moment in time I was deeply pained by events in my personal life, and teetering in and out of depression. Yet, I experienced a moment of inexplicable peace, and could not stop thinking about how painful the story was, how it seemed to explain the existence of evil in the world. I wondered if I, like the boy, was doomed. Monsieur Sviadac said nothing.

This is a rare Hassidic story in which Satan outwits the Holy One; therefore, it is of the utmost value, because it is undeniable that there are forces of evil in our world that are powerful, manipulative, and victorious. These forces are recognizable in our history, and too often in us. But something in me rebelled against this conclusion as the only interpretation of the story.

Then, over months, as the story sank deeper into me, I began to tell it to friends to relive the experience of it, to understand my inner conflict. I needed to acknowledge the harsh truth of the content of the story and also to bring forth the feeling I had of another level of meaning concealed beneath the obvious content. I began to tell it with a strange joy as if it emanated a secret light.

Malidoma Somé, a West African writer, said:

> ...when an initiated member of the community registers communication through pain, it is a signal that the soul is in need of some communion with its spiritual counterpart. In other words the soul is moving old furniture out and bringing in new furniture....We do not always allow ourselves to work through pain. More often than not we think pain is a signal that we must stop, rather than find its source. Our souls do not like stagnation....To shut down the pain is to override the call of the soul. When this happens it is a repressive measure taken against oneself, which has somber consequences.[16]

I woke up one morning with the words, "Know thyself." Perhaps, I thought, I am blinded by the stark fact that Satan wins. So I looked at the tale again, seeing all characters within myself, and realized that it was neither the Tzaddik nor the parents who were asleep, but myself. Sun Tsu, in *The Art of War*, said it is necessary for a great leader to know his enemy. However, one cannot know one's enemy until one knows oneself first. So this demanding little Hassidic tale opened the doorway within me to a greater self-knowing, and a deeper level of faith.

Discourse

In Jewish tradition it is the text of a tale, a sentence, or a single word that is studied, analyzed, compared with other stories, to draw forth from beneath its surface content a deeper significance and meaning. Such inspired commentaries are well known through the commentary of rabbis, or the Midrash. However, I am a storyteller. For me, the story is far more than the content. Meaning is illumined in the dynamic process of reciprocal telling and listening. The powerful truth of oral tradition emerges silently in the inner enactment of the story shared between listener and teller, within the story told and the story heard.

The tale begins with the birth of an unusual child to a conventional Jewish man and his wife in a village in Poland—a social world defined by traditions. The child's wild nature, inner light, and inherent longing are a threat. His innate knowing, beyond his years, cannot be dampened by prescribed disciplines. He is too inquisitive, too fresh. He refuses to bend his head to study. He faces the sky.

The little boy is the heart of us listening, who thirst for water in a dry place. No matter how deeply we've buried the rage of our heart for its own light, we all respond to the plight of the child in the tale. The place in our heart that longs to beat fearlessly and openly must know what will happen: will he succeed where we have barely been able to? From this beginning we are personally concerned.

We call into being whatever dark village streets we imagine, while we summon the wild world of the child's mind. For the child is companion to bird and beast and drawn to the forbidden friendship of the Hassidic children, who might topple the solidity of tradition and the safety of structure. We know all three within ourselves: the intuitive child, the fearful parent, and the holy madman.

The boy's insight and natural awareness is recognized and valued by the Hassidic children. He is a delight, even a revelation to his playmates, while to his parents he is a source of concern.

Their only hope is that the boy will conform. They expect that he will soon sit and study with other boys.

Then, one day, the boy is told by his playmates that he must seek a Tzaddik in another village—a Tzaddik, a holy man, a righteous man, a man whose experience is the bliss of wisdom. "He is drawn to God," the children might explain, "like water to water." The boy goes home and begs his parents, "Take me to the Tzaddik. I must see the Tzaddik."

The boy's request is a nightmare to his parents. To the listener it is a challenge, a gold nugget dangled before our eyes. Our desire is also aroused along with fear. Will he go? What will he find? We are curious to go. Will the words of the storyteller let us go now that we have heard about him? Is the Tzaddik in each of us awakened, waiting in the depths of our hearts, where he or she has always been concealed? Beneath the ordinary veneer of hearing a story we become the drama, and the cast is within us already, dressed and summoned onto the stage.

The parents refuse. They cannot allow their child to engage in something as dangerous as traveling to the Tzaddik. They cannot fan the flames of such unbridled passion. We are disappointed in them. In a story, at least, we want to visit a holy person. However, to our relief this denial strengthens the boy's resolve. He does not disappoint us. His curiosity is transformed into longing. The first denial changes him from child to pilgrim. It changes us, too—the child we imagined into being is no longer just an innocent. He is ignited, an ember burst into flame. And within us our own tamed longing is aroused and nourished.

If the story ended now, we would be left adrift. We would have to return to the dark room of our inner habitual ways of being. The light would be dimmed. The hope of gaining wisdom and freedom is reflected on the mirror of our inquisitiveness. Nonetheless, within us is a glimmer of fear. Perhaps the parents are right. At this moment we are the entire story. The fate of the boy, his parents, the Tzaddik, the Hassidic children, our own associations, is our fate. A threshold has been crossed in the hearing of the tale. It is as if we were dreaming of walking in a house and discovered another room—a room in our own house that we did not know about before, fully furnished.

Wait! We are not alone asleep, or dreaming, but awake, listening or reading, and someone is telling the story.

In *Sages and Dreamers*, Elie Wiesel reminds us, "*Aval shnayim shyoshvim.* If two persons do engage in study, the Divine Presence, the Shechinah will appear in their midst." And we, listening, drawn out of self-consciousness into the unfolding story, are not alone. Is She the one within us who listens beneath our logical mind? Is She waiting? Is it the Shechinah who burns within us? Who waits in the other village?

The boy's longing is profound. Why else would the parents finally agree to take him? It cannot be just to keep him quiet. The mother warns, "If there is the slightest sign of danger you must return immediately." Are we ready to journey no matter what happens? Or are we relieved to hear the mother's warning?

Our thinking minds are always providing opinions, warnings, judgments. Who do we believe? Which path do we follow? Shall I stay home and be safe in my nest or shall I go where my heart leads me? Do I dare? What is the risk? The storyteller leads us, holds our hands, but within us the quest occurs for each of us alone. Our fears and longings are exposed—if we can sense them. For some listeners, it is satisfactory to be a witness. To others, more easily wrenched out of moderation, the story is unnerving and the inner quest must be made. For me, the child's voice must be heard, his wish must be fulfilled.

On the journey, not far from the village, a wheel loosens on the carriage. Swiftly, the father returns. An evil omen: *A wheel becomes loose on the carriage.* The vehicle that is carrying the father and son to the encounter with either madness or holiness is perhaps not strong enough. We know that the teller knows the tale, knows that Satan is at work already.

Or is it Satan's work? When the demands of the heart are strong, are for the light, aren't we always tested and made stronger?

At the invisible level of our listening, our longing perhaps is not yet burning. We must break open even further before we can meet the Tzaddik or even recognize him or her.

The child is desperate. He wants nothing but to go to the Tzaddik. That part of us is now drawn up from a deep place of desire, and we experience intense longing. In this special circumstance of listening, we are caught off guard, unaware that we are the ground of the enactment of the story—that it is more about us than about the characters, who exist only in our imagination. We naturally release our feelings, uncover associations, connect meanings. Our seeking is uncontrived; it follows the need of the heart.

It is confusing. He is only a child. Where does such longing come from? Isn't this out of the boundary of his/our experience? No. I had forgotten how viscerally the wants of my childhood consumed me. Maybe the child is enchanted, sliding into the forbidden realm of madness. I know this madness and obsession. It has brought me the greatest of gifts and the worst suffering. His hunger is the hunger of the starving, the possessed, the one locked out of the house who cannot get warm. I want him to find the Tzaddik. I want good to conquer evil. Yet, we know the possible consequences. I found myself longing for him to meet the holy man, to satisfy my thirst for union with the divine. And can I tolerate the naked face, the piercing cry of the starving one—whom I have trained to be acceptable in the world?

Again, the parents gave in. They agreed. We know now that they love the child and do not know what to do to subdue his misery. The father takes him again. The mother warns again. I breathe quickly as I listen.

This time the wheel on the carriage does not loosen. They travel safely to the village. When they arrive at the inn (another threshold), they stop to rest, to inquire after the Tzaddik. The door is opened, but the inner door, the door made of light that will bring us face to face with the Tzaddik, is not yet approached.

A stranger enters. He sits down and they ask him, "Where do we find the Tzaddik?" In every story a stranger gives instructions; this stranger warns them away. "The Tzaddik is a madman." He satisfies all the parents' fears. He is the spoken manifestation of their hesitation, their own lack of trust. The father grabs his son and leaves. I can feel myself screaming inside, "I do not want to return. I want to go forward." But a great omen has occurred. The word of a witness informs them that the Tzaddik is truly evil. The child returns home.

What is a story if it does not provide us the opportunity to experience directly the various consequences of actions, the chance to explore the full ramifications of events? It is not for comfort that I listen, it is something inside me that calls out and draws me further into this tale. I want the truth. All the characters within me are out of the hidden corners of my imagination.

My heart beats faster. I am afraid for that part of myself. I am afraid that even in the listening I will return to my own limits. Once again I recognize the stranger in myself who judges and is afraid of leaping beyond the restrictions of my own thinking. I want the storyteller to take me on my own to the Tzaddik. "Leave them but take me," I beg. But the father takes me home. The child, it seems, is too young to go alone. The storyteller does not relieve me. I am told that the boy's health vanished. He could neither eat nor stand. He slept fitfully, falling into a fever. He lost his desire for life. Within a few weeks the little boy died.

Now I am left with the parents in this world. I am left with their utter despair and confusion. I hope the story does not end here. And it does not end here. The storyteller goes on. The father returns to the inn. He goes to the threshold himself. The fearful adult consciously goes to discover the truth.

Once again, the same stranger. Now the stranger reveals himself: "I am Satan and I kept your son from the Tzaddik."

Satan. What part of me arises in this image? Has the stranger revealed himself as the Evil One? Or is Satan a disguise? For truly, he is the teacher of uncompromising compassion. He shows me what I fear most. He reveals who the child is to me. He opens me up by breaking my heart.

I mourn the death of the child, but the listening heart has also imagined something further. For, you see, although the boy and the Tzaddik did not meet in the story, they met within me. For a moment, when the storyteller told us of the possibility of their union, the Tzaddik flickered into view where he has been waiting and the child moved toward him. This had to happen without my thinking about it, because it is beyond my comprehension. It is in the realm of mystic experience. I am not incapable of it, but I cannot conceive it, only know it. The light is so great I cannot see them—together, the Shechinah, myself, and the storyteller. And then the tale ends.

I am both humbled and empowered. In the story, Satan is victorious. Yes, it is clearly stated. However, having studied with a Vajrayana teacher of the Crazy Wisdom Lineage of Kagyu Tibetan Buddhism, I have felt how outrageous and unconventional a teacher can be to awaken the student. Thus, if I can rise for a moment over the sorrow of the tale, I ask, "What is the medicine in this death? In this story?" For in the alchemical workings of this tale, the physical child has died. What lives? When my heart was broken open, I knew their union within me. The place of longing was no longer concealed. Although the words of the story ended, the experience has occurred.

When Rabbi Hananiah was burned at the stake with the Torah, he called out to his students, "The scrolls are burning but the letters are not." Eli Wiesel wrote, "Physical tangible things come and go—not spiritual ones. They stay—suspended between heaven and earth—outside time and inaccessible to human ambitions. There is something in us mortals that is immortal."

Tikkun: Repair

My question when I first heard the story was whether evil was victorious. I asked it again and again over the next two years. I asked it because I was confronted with stories told by children caught in wars, whose life stories were as terrible as the tales of the Holocaust. I am grateful to this story, grateful that it was not easy, and that it pushed me into my pain, into acknowledging the power of evil, and beyond evil. To see that the story did not take place or end in the text or words, but in what happened in the mind of the listener and within my own heart. It bid me knock at the door of my heart, and know that it was open, and She was awake within.[17]

THE HEN AND THE ROOSTER

continues...

THE prince hid unseen until night. As soon as the princess unbound her hair, he grabbed it tight and twisted it around his arm.

She cried, "It is burning. Let it go."

He held on tighter.

She promised him the earth, the sky, the sun, the moon, the sea, and the entire world. But he did not loosen his grasp until she swore by the rooster and the hen that she would be his wife and follow him wherever he went. He made her swear again as he let loose her hair and rushed up to where she sat.

"Will you marry me?" he asked.

"I may and I may not. I too have a three-legged horse. If they do not fight, I am yours."

The king's son agreed, forgetting the instructions from the old man. The two three-legged horses were set loose together. They gently rubbed against each other's necks and whinnied happily. In truth they were mother and son and pleased to find one another again. The prince and the woman with the two birds set off on the backs of their horses to begin their journey.

Another Way of Knowing

The World of an Epic Singer

Here's a long night—an endless night—before us,
And no time yet for sleep, not in this hall.
Recall the past deeds and the strange adventure.
I could stay up all night until the sacred Dawn
As long as you might wish to tell your story.

—Homer, The Odyssey

*W*HEN I WAS A child I longed to be carried away by a story. I imagined tents, fire, courts, and markets where exotic storytellers gathered. I would march outside onto the streets of Brooklyn in search of such a place only to return home disappointed. My mother, guardian of stories, music, and the secrets of Rumanian cooking, comforted me. "You can go there in your play, or in your dreams." I was not satisfied. I sat under the grand piano in our living room and pretended that I was in a caravan, or a tent. I had a great longing.

It is not surprising. In this time of global, often impersonal communication, we are thirsty for ways of knowing that support the spiritual sustenance and direct experience that storytelling at its best provides.

A thousand years after Homer wrote down the once-oral epic of *The Odyssey*, we are still not bored by the adventures of its hero, Odysseus. He journeys for us. We are moved reading it, or seeing it enacted on stage or in film. However, in reality, such passive renditions are a mere shadow of having heard the story told and sung. Homer's bard reminds us that "there is no boon in life more sweet" than to *hear* the story.

In the court of King Alkinoos of Phoenicia, where the bard sang his tale, there was no book; there was no TV, no tape to stop or rewind. All images were generated uniquely in the imagination of each listener, not limited to one author's or director's projection. The power of this sweet bondage arose from a single voice and the sound of a harp. Each listener was riveted in timeless attention. Awareness was everything, for to fall asleep was to lose the thread of the story. The audience's well-being depended on Odysseus' safe return because while listening, everyone had become this epic hero. And what made it even more intense was that the hero whose tale was told was listening to his own story.

Fundamentally, an epic is a story that brings to life the birth, adventure, and death of a hero, whose exploits exemplify the most valued human qualities. In *The Hero with a Thousand Faces*, Joseph Campbell explains that the epic is a transition between myths (the profound, symbolic tales of creation) and the appearance of human history. "History is no longer carried forward by timeless mythological processes," Campbell writes, "but by the heroes, more or less human in character, through whom the world destiny is realized."

Many of the world's great epic stories, which are no doubt

familiar to you, have been recorded in fixed or literary versions: *The Odyssey* from Greece, *Gilgamesh* from the ancient Middle East, *Beowulf* from England, *The Ramayana* and *The Mahabharata* from India, *The Popul Vuh* from Mexico, *Gesar of Ling* from Tibet, to mention only a few.

But the key to activating the essential power in myth and story lies in the listening. As Margaret Mead warned, we must not lose access to a "fertile imagination" which is kept alive by a "dynamic listening." It is the master teller of tales who is trained to create the ground for such heightened listening and imaginative response. Thus, it is the very process of being engaged in a story (particularly an epic tale) that empowers us, not the content of the story alone. Because our literate society is unused to the power of the incanted word sung by an authentic epic singer, it is easy to overlook the role of the performer who, in a reciprocal creative relationship with an audience, generates deep levels of meaning and feeling in the heart and mind of each listener.

We know little about epic singers. Scholars have mainly devoted themselves to a study of the story and the performances as analyzable texts or events. Epic singing as a profound tradition is fading from the earth as cultures change. Most such performances have been reduced to little more than entertainment.

But the role of an epic singer in his or her culture is much more than that of an entertainer. As Qahhor Rakhimor, an epic singer from Uzbekistan, explains, "To be a good storyteller one must know the words, the music, the instrument, and the song. But if one is not inspired by God, it is mere entertainment."

Epic singers (female and male) are philosophers, historians, spiritual leaders, oral poets, musicians, mediators, experts in human nature, teachers, and masters of ceremony. They are capable of engendering a powerful and thorough attention. They are rigorously trained in ways of knowing that produce compassion and wisdom.

I had the privilege of meeting Almas Almatov, an epic singer from the vast steppes of Kazakhstan in Central Asia, thanks to an unusual Kazakh woman, Alma Kunanbaeva, whom I had met six years earlier in a classroom of the Performance Studies Department of New York University. Alma's firsthand knowledge and understanding of the artists and their true worth surpasses most scholars'. For over twenty-five years she has single-handedly helped perpetuate the tradition of epic singers, or zhyraus.

Alma had been invited by my friend Zev Feldman, a scholar of ethnomusicology and oral epic, to give a lecture on the epic singers of Kazakhstan, her native land. She spoke in Russian. A female Soviet scholar translated her rhythmic, lively language into monotonous English. My eyes and ears quickly became allergic to the limited translation, but I drank in the presence of this vibrant Kazakh woman.

Her first sentence could not be mistranslated: "The epic singer joins heaven and earth." Alma Kunanbaeva was revealing thoughts I only had in dreams. She played a tape of epic singers she had recorded in Kyzl Orda. I recognized the story, but this was wonderfully different.

Long hidden to us as a Soviet nation, Kazakhstan maintains the tradition of the epic singers as the most important mode of artistic and cultural expression. The vitality of the living tradition of bards is one reason the Kazakh people have maintained their culture in the face of generations of political invasions and domination. But even in his own country, Almas Almatov is unique. He has been trained traditionally, but he also sought out a Western education so that his art could move into the twenty-first century.

"Almas Almatov was born into a society that supported his role," Zev Feldman explained. "The Kazakh oral tradition had—and still has—a central function in defining the identity of the Kazakh people. Between the fifteenth and eighteenth centuries the zhyraus were advisors to the khans [rulers]."

As a child, Zev continued, Almas was chosen because he was extremely intelligent and showed ability at music and memorization, and a love of story. He also had prophetic dreams that showed his talents and connection to the ancestors. Taken from his playmates, Almas was tested through hours of rigorous study, listening, and competitions so that his technique was constantly improved.

This reminded me of a friend, a griot from the Gambia, now living in New York, who explained that from eight years old until eleven he was kept awake listening to his grandfather sing the great epics of his tribe for nine or ten hours until they had infiltrated his mind.

The city of Kyzl Orda (where Almas now lives) in West Kazakhstan, is between the Syr Daria River and the Aral Sea. Until the 1930s, Kazakhstan was primarily a nomadic pastoral society. The epics were formed in that milieu. Zev reminded me, "Their values also embody certain principles of social interaction which have universal significance. Almas is a master of this knowledge."

His is a legacy of a past that is always changing and relevant in the present. Looking at the stories as living events rather than as texts or scripts, he sees they are ultimately about what is evoked in the heart and mind of each listener guided by the bard. The experience of the telling urges knowledge into inherent wisdom more inclusive than explanation.

To sense the living presence of the epic singer is not possible in film or recordings. His or her face-to-face relationship with an audience is incomparable. It is my hope that the story of that meeting will evoke the power of the experience of the epic singer, provoke a longing to hear a story well told, and open a discussion on the treasure of knowledge housed in the heart of the bard, a treasure that must be protected and perpetuated for all our sakes.

In the fall of 1995, Zev and I invited Alma for a weekend in New York City. Ben Haggarty, director of storytelling festivals in England and Wales, was there as well. A storyteller with a deep regard for the tradition of the epic singer, Ben was nurtured by his grandfather's respect for the bards he met in Turkey at the turn of the century. A pioneer in the telling of epic tales in English, he has created a magnificent international storytelling festival held in an eleventh-century Welsh castle each year. Upon learning more of the important work of Almas Almatov from Alma, Ben decided to feature the celebrated zhyrau in his 1996 festival.

On July 1st, shortly after arriving at Ben's London home, I walked into his kitchen for a glass of water. A man was seated at the table. He had the look of a Brooklyn butcher and the presence of a king. He exuded confidence and grace. He had a round, handsome face, both masculine and gentle. Thick-armed, posture upright, dressed in a Western short-sleeved cotton shirt and dark pants, he was completely natural. In all my conversations with Alma about him, I had not really imagined him. Now, seeing him, I felt I could never ignore his presence in my life, even if I was never to travel to Central Asia. It was as if I had already made the trip. I knew immediately that this was Almas.

The next night there was a presentation by the epic singers at London's Royal Festival Hall. Before the performance Almas was intensified, his energy rising slowly to the surface. Silent, he seated himself apart, preparing. He was watching the way hawks watch from a distance, preparing for flight, locating their prey.

I sat down and waited with the audience in the theater. The lights dimmed. Alma came on stage first. At first she spoke in her shaky English too rapidly. Then suddenly, when the strings of energy and thoughts seemed dispersed, she caught them up again and spun several short stories and anecdotes about bards. These were her gold threads. "All the songs of the Bards were sung by Korkut, the prophet, the shaman, the first storyteller. A bard must know death. An epic singer joins heaven and earth. He is the tongue, the eyes, the nose, the heart of his people."

She stood on the stage like a cowgirl, fierce and somewhat wild, with the flamboyant beauty of a much younger woman. Slowly, the entire theater was transformed. She was creating an oasis for Almas to enter.

Then she introduced Almas Almatov. He walked on stage dressed like a wizard from a book of stories. His hat was black and pointed, with swirls and flowers, and his dark, woolen robe was embroidered in white. His smile was broad.

He sat down—no, plunked down—on a pillow with force and began speaking to Alma in Kazakh. They conversed on stage as if we were not there. He asked questions about what she had said in her introduction (Zev translated in my ear as they spoke). When he was ready, and felt into her spoken stories, Almas looked around, his eyes swooping over the theater, taking us in, assessing us.

Then he made a joke. Alma translated. I don't recall the words, yet it was disarming. It relaxed us, made us ready. Without hesitation he strummed the dombra (lute), urgent, lucid, rhythmic notes. He began to sing, his nasal voice piercing the air like an arrow. I have never heard such a sound—not pleasant and comforting, but slicing and rich.

My heart opened. I sat up to listen with my entire body. Alma sat down. She was changed, calmed. She listened in her own language, more than Kazakh words and songs, a language of birds and deer and earth. Her head moved, her arms moved. She became a graceful hieroglyph of listening.

Almas was a magician, a king, a confident woman, a doctor operating on our minds. No one cared that we did not understand the words of the story. The sound of his voice and his presence bound our spines to the sky that until that moment had been covered by a ceiling. The black earth seemed to be under our feet. What was this music that rendered me alive and vibrating? Occasionally Zev gave us hints of what was taking place in the story.

I remembered Alma's words: "The epic singer knows life and death. Joins heaven and earth."

Sometimes it is said that the true power of the storyteller is the ability to take you elsewhere, make you forget where you are, to drive away the present. But here I was transported out of the fantasy of my thoughts into an abiding present.

Afterwards, backstage, Almas was breathing hard. He held

his hands out. We embraced like old friends and he spoke to me. I didn't understand a single word. I gave him figs to nibble, offerings.

There was a dinner reception in another building. We walked, exhilarated, refreshed by the performance, the moonlight, the river Thames. Arm in arm, Alma and Almas strolled ahead of me, able to walk in two worlds at once.

The last day before leaving Ben's house for Wales, Almas insisted that we all gather in the kitchen. He called for Ben's father, the oldest man. Then Almas blessed the house, the father, the wife, the children, Ben, all of us, and reminded us of closings and gratitude. We were children compared to this man, who in reality was younger than we were. For each of us he composed a poem precisely offering what we needed at the moment.

In Wales I had the chance to watch the magic again and again as Western audiences were stunned into exquisite attention whenever Almas walked upon the stage. It was an enchanting event on the magnificent grounds of a castle on the Bristol Channel. We sat in large tents in the jousting field, on the grass in several gardens, and in smaller colorful tents dotted throughout the field. All weekend long storytellers and musicians from all over the world performed, conversed, or wandered about milling with the audience. This annual event honoring storytellers and epic singers is sponsored by the St. Donat's Art Center in South Glamorgan, Wales, near the town of Llantwit Major. It was well worth the long journey.

Over the next few days, Zev and I spent as much time with Almas as we could to benefit from his experience as an epic singer in a living culture. In an interview Ben asked him what he thought his role was at present. Almas responded, "As a zhyrau it is necessary to be an expert in your people's history, to have great dignity, to gain knowledge about human life through deep thinking and analyzing about one's own life; and it is necessary to have a good education."

Almas considers that his most essential task is to teach, and to preserve traditional ways of knowing based on holistic learning and a high level of simultaneous intellectual and intuitive awareness between generations. "My commitment is to make the zhyraus strong from the root to the flower to the top of the tree. In the West you have so many ideals, changing all the time like waves of the ocean. My tradition makes me a rock."

Almas returned to Kyzl Orda to continue his mission. He has a school where the whole person of the bard is trained. Already there have been thirty-two graduates, and over one hundred bards performing in Kazakhstan.

Ben remained in England, and Alma, Zev, and I returned to America. Each of us was inspired and provoked by our meeting with Almas in the U.K. Each of us was encouraged to take back what we had learned to apply to our own work in our own worlds.

So much happened during those days that I was barely able to assimilate it. One night I asked for a dream. I dreamed that I was walking through hallways hearing the voices of an old Rumanian man and woman singing Jewish songs. My tape recorder would not work. I said to myself, "I will not forget this." Then I was standing in a church. A priest showed me a plate. I looked closer and said to him, "I know that plate. It was once a Seder plate."

I told the dream to Zev Feldman. He laughed out loud, reminding me that the Seder plate, the ritual plate for the Passover supper, was used as a memory device to recall the events of the Passover story, the only epic in the Bible, the story of the Exodus. A heroic tale of an outer journey, the escape from slavery to freedom, and an inner journey of liberation.

Here we close our story; good fortune to you!

Whoever tells this tale to others becomes free

and does not have to labor painfully for his food.

I carry the names Rama and Sita seated within

an amulet when I travel over the world, and I keep

it in my house when I am home. It lets me go in

peace and return safely to those who love me.

—The Ramayana

THE HEN AND THE ROOSTER

continues...

UNFORTUNATELY, they had tarried too long. The bald-headed lute player awoke, and saw them riding away. He rose from his cloud, and seized the maiden with the birds. Then he flew up toward the sky and vanished.

The prince begged the two three-legged horses for help. The stirrups of the horses turned into servants who bound him with ropes to the spot where the maiden had been taken.

After a short time he grew impatient so he unbound himself and walked onwards until he came to another meadow. In the meadow there were three other three-legged horses grazing. One was black as night; one was red as dawn; and the third shone like gold. The black horse was the messenger of death. If someone were to mount it, it would knock the rider against the rocks. If someone mounted the red horse, he was carried to another land within the earth. The white horse was the messenger of light. Whoever mounted that horse would be carried into the sky.

The king's son tried to catch the black horse but could not. Nor could he catch the white horse. However, he succeeded in catching the red horse. He rode downward for a long time until he arrived in an unknown and distant kingdom within the earth. He dismounted and the horse rose back to the world above.

But make no mistake: every image or almost every image conceals a symbol, like the bait in a trap, and behind the symbol lies an idea which may be very complex....In the apparently naive guise of a fairy-tale, the initiatory story calls for the disciple's constant attention and for astonishing intellectual gymnastics in solitary meditation in order to extract from it the "substantive marrow."

AMADOU HAMPATE BA

Misfortune's Fortune

$\mathcal{S}$HIVA AND PARVATI'S STORYTELLING conversations on Mount Kailas often began when Shiva, God of Creation and Dissolution, was questioned by his wife Parvati about the origins of a particular individual's fate. In one of her many manifestations of the Great Goddess she lured him into telling her how, through an action many lifetimes ago, a particular person began the karmic journey that has now made them who they are. "Shiva, you who know the past, the present, and the future, please narrate to me the history of that beggar." Since Shiva is the Lord of Time and lost time is no time at all, he stopped time and whispered in her seashell of an ear, "Long ago that beggar, who has been an ant, a thief, an elephant, and a woman, was the great King of Benares. He loved his Queen and suffered from extreme jealousy. One day..."

The ceaseless conundrum of whether one is predestined or somehow the author of a particular fortune or fate seems impossible to solve through human logic. Any explanation is limited to how I tell or hear the story. What religion did I grow up with, or what philosophy have I come to adopt? How far back can I trace the cause, effect, or ultimate sources of a particular incident? How vast is my perception? If I am fated, can I change my fate? Does it matter what I do, or will the story still end in the same way?

Once, in Taipei, I was brought to a famous astrologer. He reported to my hostess, in Chinese, the fated date when I would discover I had a serious illness. She was reluctant to present me with the details of his reading; she had hoped it to be a source of delight for me. However, she gave me the date and made certain that I understood that I would die of something else much later in life. The date of my death was left unspoken. On the date he predicted, August 3, 1989 (the anniversary of my own mother's death), I was told that I had cancer. Which was my fate: the actual date of the illness; the unconscious personal memory of the anniversary of my mother's death; or an uncanny coincidence? Perhaps all of the above. Or none. But it is a good story.

....

Once upon a time, there was a king and queen in Spain who lost their fortune. Why and how is not told. They became beggars living in a hovel with their seven children. One day, while searching for food, the queen was told by an old woman in a market, "I know the cause of your misfortune. It is your youngest child. Get rid of her and all will be well again." The queen said, "That is not possible." The old woman cackled, "If you look at your children while they sleep, you will note that six sleep with their arms tucked beneath their heads or shoulders, but the seventh sleeps with her arms crossed over her heart." Annoyed, the queen departed. Curious, she watched her children asleep that night, and saw that indeed the youngest girl slept with her arms crossed over her heart.

The little girl awoke and asked her mother what was wrong. The queen said, "An old woman told me something I did not believe." When she related the incident her daughter answered, "If I should be the cause of your trouble then I cannot stay. I will go out into the world and seek my fortune." The child left that night.

If it was the child's fate to make this journey, then the old woman provided good news (as you will soon see). We can never know what would have happened had she stayed, because she did not. Just as in our own lives we can bemoan what should or could have happened had we done such and such instead of what we did, we can never find that answer. Of course there could be another variant to the story. In this case, it ends differently in versions from Greece, Italy, and Iran.

....

The Great Rebbi Zusia of Anapoli prayed every morning before breakfast, "God, please provide me with food today." His servant grew angry at his stupidity. "Why does he pray to God for food? I am the one who brings him cakes and tea every morning." So the servant decided not to bring the food the next day. Early the next morning the Rebbi set off for the Shul before dawn dressed in his ragged coat and worn boots. Crossing a bridge, he fell into the mud. A man, thinking he was no doubt a good-for-nothing thief, turned away and did not help him. However, the man felt guilty afterward and inquired from a merchant whether he knew this vagabond who had fallen in the mud.

The merchant said, "It is the Rebbi. He is a Tzaddik, a Holy Man. He cares nothing for the adornments of this world." Ashamed, the man decided to make amends by bringing the Rebbi his breakfast. The servant was astonished when immediately after the Rebbi's prayer a man brought fresh cakes and tea to the door of the house. "It can be no other than God who answers his prayer," concluded the servant.

....

Whether he would have received food had he not prayed or fallen in the mud is something I can't address because that is not told in the story. As for the little girl:

When she sought work, it was interrupted by her ill fortune. As she guarded the cloths of a tailor, a wind blew the cloths asunder and she lost her job. When she worked in a bakery, thieves plundered the shop. "You are nothing but trouble," she was told.

Flying from New York to Seattle, I sat next to a nervous, handsome man. We began conversing, and I asked at some point, as one can do in an airplane or a taxi, "Why are you anxious?" He answered without hesitation, "Because I am doomed." With three more hours left on our journey, I told him the ancient Egyptian story of "The Doomed Prince."

....

At the birth of a prince, the Seven Hathors, or Fates, predicted that he was doomed to be killed by a dog, a snake, or a crocodile. To avert his fate, his father, the king, built a thick-walled palace in the middle of a desert. His son was brought up protected from dogs, snakes, and crocodiles. At some point, the boy climbed to the parapet to look beyond his confinement, and saw an old man walking with a greyhound puppy. His longing for the little dog was so extreme that at last the King, thinking a puppy could bring no harm, agreed to buy one for his son. The dog became the prince's most faithful companion. When the prince came of age he extracted the story of his doom from his servant, and chose to leave with his dog and face his fortune, no matter the outcome.

....

The story is long and marvelous. Through winning a leaping contest, he comes to marry a princess in Upper Egypt and takes his place as a prince once again. He reveals to his wife the prophecy of his doom. Soon after, while he is sleeping, she sees a snake slither through a crack in the wall of his bedroom and kills it, saving him from that fate. However, later that afternoon his dog escapes. The prince rushes after him. The dog dives into the river Nile where it is attacked by a crocodile. To save the dog, the prince leaps into the river.

The dog survives and stands barking as the prince battles with the crocodile. There the story ends. One is never told whether the prince is killed by the crocodile, defeats it to be later killed by the dog, or overcomes his fate entirely. It is left to the listener. I asked the man beside me how he would end the story. He answered with gloomy certainty, "He is doomed like me. The crocodile will devour him." The woman seated on the other side of me, who obviously had listened to the tale, said, "I think he defeats the crocodile and returns to his wife."

The girl in Spain took a job washing shirts for a washerwoman; she gave her name as Misfortune. The prince who employed them was pleased with the cleanliness of his shirts and rewarded the washerwoman.

The washerwoman took fresh bread to the oceanside each day. She explained to Misfortune that she was offering her appreciation to her Fortune. When Misfortune accompanied her she saw a lovely young woman in a clean, flowing gown arise from the water to accept the bread. She inquired, "Do I also have a Fortune?" The washerwoman uneasily explained, "Your Fortune can be found further down the beach beside a pile of garbage." Misfortune found her Fortune—a filthy, angry, misshapen hag who muttered and spat and refused the bread. Day after day the girl returned, gaining the trust of her Fortune, until at last, when the hag grabbed the bread, she grabbed the hag. She dragged her Fortune into the ocean and washed her, removed her filthy clothes, combed her hair, and dressed her in spotless new clothes. Her Fortune was transformed. It was then that the Fortune renamed the girl Goodfortune.

The Fortune gave her a gift which ultimately led Goodfortune to marry the prince whose shirts she'd washed. Years later, a gold carriage arrived at her palace. Her mother, once again the Queen of Spain, embraced her saying, "Indeed you were the cause of our misfortune. As soon as you left everything improved, and we were given back our castle. However, my heart was ill at ease until the moment when I saw you again." And they all lived happily ever after.

....

One last story, from Armenia.

....

A man who set out to find his fortune made a long journey to a certain wise hermit. Along the way he met a starving wolf, a beautiful unmarried woman in distress, and a dried-up tree growing beside a river. He promised to ask the hermit advice for them as well.

He was told, "Your fortune is asleep. Go home and wake it up," and was given answers to his other questions as well. Hurrying home, he advised the tree that it was dry because there was a pot of gold buried beneath it that blocked its roots. The tree begged him to dig up the gold, which he did. Having no use for gold, the tree offered it to the man, who turned down the gold, saying he was in a hurry to go home and wake his fortune. He reported to the woman that she was lonely because she had not met a kind companion. The woman asked the man to marry her. He refused, saying he had to race home and wake his luck.

Finally he came upon the wolf and explained how he had dug up the gold and spoken to the woman. The wolf asked, "What did the hermit say about my fortune?" The man replied, "The hermit said you should find a foolish man and eat him up and you would never be hungry again." So the wolf ate the man.

....

When Shiva finished his story to Parvati, she asked, "Will the beggar become a king again in the future?" Shiva did not answer. Smiling alluringly, Parvati asked, "Was that story true?" The destroyer answered, moving his lips from her ear, "One can only know whether a story is true from the voice of the storyteller." Shiva began time again and disappeared. Parvati returned to her meditations as Uma, the young daughter of the Mountain.

THE HEN AND THE ROOSTER

continues . . .

A LONE, the prince walked until he came to a town. An old woman sat at the gate of the town. He asked her for water. She said, "I would give you water but a dragon owns our only well. Every day it demands a person. Today the king's daughter will be sacrificed."

"Give me a pitcher and I will bring you water."

"You are a fool. The dragon will kill you," she said.

"It is true that I am a fool," said the prince.

He took the pot from the old woman's arms and set off. By the well sat a young woman dressed in black.

"Sister, you do not need to be devoured by the dragon."

"Leave me alone," she begged.

"For the moment," he said and lay down to rest because he was tired.

When the dragon appeared in the sky above the well, the princess tried to wake the prince. He did not wake up until he felt three of her tears on his cheek.

What a year may not bring, an hour might.

—ROMA PROVERB

A Language of No Words

Translation

$\mathcal{T}$HE DAY I FIRST met the Roma women it was the middle of a harsh Moldavian winter. We sat in an unheated room in a city called Bacau, in Romania. Leslie Hawke had asked if I would tell stories. She was the director of a remarkable project (ovidiu.rom)—taking Gypsy women and children off the streets where they were begging, to give the mothers work and better living skills, and sending their children to classes to prepare for school.

The women sat in a circle, huddled close for warmth. Their arms were tightly held against their bodies like the adolescents who confront me with suspicion in Manhattan high schools. My translator was a therapist, Daniela Cornestean, whom I had worked with for two years in a more northern city. We had developed a magnificent dance of translation from the first summer of our project with teenagers in the peasant village of Malini to our work with orphans in the city of Iasi. Daniela's English was excellent and her listening so immediate that she had discovered a way to turn my sentences into Romanian without interrupting the flow of relationship between myself and listeners.

I decided to tell a story about my Grandma Ida and the stories she had told me about growing up in the mud-thick town of Lomza in Poland when she was a child. The unspoken backdrop to her story was the sorrow of anti-Semitism that provoked her to travel to American in 1900, at the age of sixteen. I was aware of the racism against the Gypsies. Before World War II they lived side by side with Jews in the cities where I now worked. I wondered if this connection was meaningful as the mothers leaned toward me ever so slightly to listen.

Daniela's translation beneath my words was like a musician's accompaniment. There were long pauses and sometimes almost simultaneous language. We had learned that the gestures, the feeling, the breath, the rhythm, the reception of images and events all need a certain intuitive timing and space to move back and forwards between us and the audience: a triangle of attention.

At the start I was aware of Daniela's struggle to concentrate and of my own short sentences to make certain we would fall into the tempo of communication that depended not only on us but the women in the circle. They never revealed any interest with their eyes, so I avoided making eye contact. Yet, I could feel the shift in the air in the room and saw their strongly-gripped arms loosen. The hard wall of distrust melted somewhat as they made their way into the story that they imagined.

Perhaps it provided associations for them. Childhood, death, magic, mothers, food, old languages, gardens, and memories— the stuff of everyone's remembrances.

There were sentences I spoke mimicking Ida's singsong Yiddish accent. I used Yiddish words. Daniela had to ask me what they meant. I translated for her. She translated for them. They laughed when I acted like my grandmother, bending my body ever so slightly, feeling the weight and age of her immigrant body that seemed always in another world—as if she was baked in Polish foods and sounds and memories. Her voice held an entire universe of languages. Ida spoke Yiddish and Polish. She also knew Russian, German, and French. She incanted a weird version of English that I adored and imitated when I was a child. There were so many stories she never told. The few details I had, now spun into the fabric of this story, were filled with a sense of something I could not grasp. I wondered if that yearning was fragrant in the sound of my voice. I had no way of knowing.

I asked about their own childhood memories. I asked for a description of a place they recalled. Those who chose to respond gave very curt answers, a few women turned away. Daniela repeated the question. Answers began: "We had a garden in front of the house where my mother grew vegetables." "My grandmother lived in a wooden house. Her hair was black even when she was old." "The place I liked was a shed behind the house." "The kitchen was outdoors."

A woman signaled with her hand for me to come closer. I got up and kneeled before her. I watched her eyes. Daniela translated: "We went to a meadow in the summer. There were fires and lots of talking." The space between our words was alive. Just as I had watched the mothers speak to Daniela, they now all watched me listen to Daniela, watching the woman who described the wind in the trees and the sound of a horse neighing. A language of no words passed between us. I repeated what Daniela said to me in English out loud to render each image into sound. I was mapping their stories in space with my voice. They shook their heads. Eyes widened.

"What do you think?" I whispered to Daniela. She said, "They are enjoying themselves. Look at their feet." I saw their feet were extended, no longer hidden under the chairs. She was translating gestures. "I think there is trust," she added.

Then an older woman, harshly thin and unbearably sad, obviously once beautiful, whose hair was covered in a traditional red headscarf, uncrossed her arms. "My father told me stories." She gestured, one finger circling in the air. "I do not remember the stories. I remember the circle of white smoke in the dark room, smoke around his lips that warmed the space we sat in." Daniela asked her a question for clarification and then repeated this fragment of memory to me. I felt I had been let into a house of few details, longing as I longed for my grandmother's past. But she said that was all she remembered.

It was the way it was said that moved me. I heard more than the words but could never explain what I heard. The image of the man's lips, of the intimacy between father and daughter, and of the white smoke in the dark. It was a tale of a time and a world that had passed for her. Perhaps for all time.

I was a rider on a three-legged horse going slowly, not sure of reaching a destination. In fact, I know that my strength lay in my *not* having a destination, of accepting that I was a stranger. A preconceived expectation about what a story was and what I wanted to know or hear would have meant I sought something and was not willing to know them as they were. I was Gadje (a white person), who had no language and no knowledge. So my relationship birthed in the process of translation, where the awkward spaces gave us presence in otherness and a chance to slow down.

I explained that I was the granddaughter of a Romanian Jewish woman who was the wife of a Grand Rabbi. She had died when I was six months old. I offered them my tenuous connection to their history. One woman had been to Dorohoi, the area of Mahlia's birth. "There is a Tsigan village nearby that had previously been mostly Jewish." Another woman told me about a Jewish family where her father worked: "They lived on the street where we are now, before the war." She described a tiled wood heater in the living room. Conversation eased our connection.

What happened in the two hours of our meeting could have happened in a half-hour if I spoke Romanian and was alone. But because of my ignorance and my dependence on translation I was able to be present with them in a way that was deeper than the exact words that were being shared. The attempt to engage with each other was bigger. I could be honestly not knowing, which became another kind of knowing, the translation of silence and seeing into genuine meeting.

As the women were getting up to leave, I asked if they liked the storytelling. A few of the women stayed. The others were racing in their thin boots back onto the snow-covered street to catch a train to Buhusi, twenty minutes away, where their families waited.

A large woman, wearing an oversized and faded Michael Jackson t-shirt said, "I liked it because I forgot about my problems. I remembered that in my childhood I was happy."

Our time together was about remembering that joy could be recalled. It was not lost as they had feared. I responded in Romanian, "Multsomesc...Thank you." My mispronunciation brought laughter from the group that was left.

"Will you come again?" asked a woman, surprising me in English. She was young and looked like a Gypsy girl of my imagination. She was one of the characters who rode in the caravan beneath my piano.

"I hope so. If I can come back, what would you want to do?"

She answered in Romanian to one of the staff standing nearby, who repeated it in Romanian to Daniela, who repeated her words to me. "We want to tell stories to our children. We want to remember our hearts. Our lives are very hard." She spoke for herself and the others.

I asked if the women knew their Roma language. "Most do not," said Narcissa. "Do you know Tsigan stories?" I asked. "No," she answered in English. Then she told me that her grandmother had been a traditional Roma. She showed me her silver rings and a silver bracelet, hand crafted, and told me a story about her grandmother giving them to her because "I am a real Gypsy," she boasted.

I spent the next six months traveling back and forth to Bacau under an Open Society grant to give storytelling workshops. I wanted to have Daniela translate, but it was not always possible. The staff volunteered, but they did not repeat what they heard in totality. They did not respect the women. It was obvious when it was not accurate or even close to what was being said. I learned to listen to the sounds of the mothers' voices more deeply, as if I could hear the feeling behind the words. It became as much a project to work with the translators, Romanian therapists born into suspicion of Gypsies, as the work with the women.

I discovered in those times how much of a story is never spoken, and how true listening has as much to do with trust and sensing as with the literal meaning of sentences.

On one of our last days, we returned to the question of their childhood memories. I asked again for descriptions of precious places. This time they began to tell me stories, long stories, about their lives. The constant engagement in making stories had expanded their vocabulary of memory. When it was over, the women who had denied being Roma, denied knowing their language, all conspired in a moment of inspiration to give me a gift.

One woman stood up. She clapped her hands. The others stood up behind her. She began to sing an old song in an old language. Keeping the beat with their beaten-down shoes, the other women sang behind her. Their beauty was the beauty of being. No one in the room understood the meaning of the Roma words anymore and there was no need for translation.

A good person will find a treasure even in poverty.
A fool will find no luck even with wealth.

—Roma proverb

THE HEN AND THE ROOSTER

continues . . .

THEN, he shot an arrow that pierced the dragon's belly. Water poured from its body. The prince rushed away to avoid the flood, and fell asleep on the other side of the growing lake. The princess returned home. The king, her father, was astonished. He sent ervants to search for the youth who had saved his daughter.

They found him asleep and dragged him to the palace. Afraid he would have to marry the princess in that world and never find the maiden with the two birds, he grabbed a hare on the road and put it in his pocket. When he arrived at the palace the king rewarded him with his daughter's hand in marriage. The prince refused.

"He saved my life, but I do not want to marry a man with a rabbit in his pocket," the princess said to her father.

The king agreed. "What do you want?" he asked the prince.

"I want to find a way to return home. I am betrothed to a princess who was carried away by a bald-headed lute player."

If I don't burn, where will the light come from?

—Nizam Hikmet

Natural Interruptions

THE ESSENTIAL KNOWLEDGE IS that we are not separate. We are entwined as if with invisible threads with each other, ancestors, and the natural world. At the forefront of mythic thinking is this knowing. There is no more serious business than remembering, acknowledging, and protecting the awareness that there is an inherent sacred bond and responsibility between human beings and nature. From this awareness arise meaning, equanimity, and compassion.

In the ongoing dance of spirit and matter, ceaselessly manifesting as the play of the world, there are constant reminders, ordinary and unusual. However, without awareness, the concept of interdependence does not penetrate. Explanations, information, or statistics alone, no matter how shocking, have little transformative power. They are dry seeds thrown on dry earth. Only direct experience of the truth of our mutuality can change our minds, allowing us to throw off the burden of habits that leave us exiled in the state of forgetting.

The following tales, quotes, and incidents are offered as clues and inspiration.

. . .

Recently, on Third Avenue in Manhattan, a lime-green flying insect the size of my thumb stopped a horde of rushing people in mid-conversation. "Ugh!" "Help." "Disgusting." "Get it away from me!" One person after another screamed, then brushed away the alien creature. It was an invasion from the natural world.

The insect flew to the street. A young man in black boots lifted his foot to crush the little monster. "Awful. I'll kill it!"

Suddenly, as if I had heard my own forgotten language in a foreign land, I blocked the black boot. I gathered the green insect in my hands and ran to find a garden, saying, "I don't mean to frighten you. I am looking for a place to put you." It grew still. I found a small clump of grass surrounding a tree and let the insect free.

I knew it was a futile act. Yet the insect was alive and beautiful, as vivid as a full moon suddenly appearing in a foggy sky—or a smile in a crowded subway. The natural interruption awoke the wilderness inside me; I was sorrowful and grateful.

. . .

All of us carry within ourselves something that is waiting for the right moment when it can burst out and repair the particular separation that we are experiencing....Nature is still alive in us, and that is why we feel we are in exile.

—Malidoma Somé,
The Healing Wisdom of Africa

. . .

Louis Bird, an Omushkego (Cree) elder, living on the Hudson Bay in Canada, not far from his tribal birthplace, painstakingly and alone collected stories and histories of elders for the last thirty years. He speaks both English and Cree. He explained, 'When I walk on Omushkego land, I walk on two paths." He knows the ancient myths and legends of place and people told over thousands of years, as well as the names given to places in the last century by white settlers. "But my grandchildren will only walk on one path," he said. That is why he is collecting the stories.

. . .

Waiting for a subway at the Union Square station is an immersion in disturbance. It is only tolerable because we are accustomed to it, numbed by the engulfing familiarity of noise and smell.

One day, a train pulled up to the platform. The doors opened and I entered a silent subway car. A net of fresh crabs lay abandoned on the floor. I leaped over them and looked up. No one smiled or nodded to acknowledge my weird dilemma. Then the visceral sense of communion touched me, impossible to ignore. I took a seat and leaned into the atmosphere.

For a moment my eyes met the eyes of a fisherman in a dark blue jacket and a navy wool cap. Then he looked away, his eyes glazing over. He had a crab in his right pocket.

He started sobbing, "Mary." He wailed her name again and again. That grief, so unfiltered and public, was like an earthquake or a huge whale too close to a boat. It pierced the heart of the people on the subway and returned us all to nature. When I went outside, I saw everything clearly.

. . .

A hunter in Japan could find no ducks. He went to a sacred lake, thinking himself safe because he was alone and unseen, although it was forbidden to hunt there. A male and female duck swam out of the reeds together. He killed the male duck, took it home, and had it for dinner.

That night a woman appeared in his dreams weeping inconsolably. Trembling, he woke to find her beside the bed. "Why did you kill my husband? Tomorrow morning return to the lake and see the consequences of your action." As the sun rose, he returned to the lake. The duck swam out from the reeds and before his eyes, she bent her graceful neck and with her beak she tore herself open and died. He never hunted again.

. . .

The unexpected and the incredible belong in this world.
Only then is life whole.

—C.G. Jung

. . .

In Chinatown I saw a woman chasing hundreds of tiny turtles down the street. They had gotten loose from a tank in her market stall. Everyone on the street walked carefully and slowly, not harming a single one.

. . .

May 1. The sound of doves brought me to the kitchen at the back of my house on Broadway. *Whoo Hoo. Whoo Hoo.* My three cats strolled quickly toward the window. Outside, a pair of gray doves sat cooing on the window sill. We sat together, the three cats and me, watching and listening to the birds beyond the glass window singing their wild song in the city. So other, so near.

. . .

Natural interruptions in our lives, experienced in events or through the heightened state of attention we bring to story, cut through our ignorance and imagined separateness. In that space of tender heart, broken apart—mind aware before thought— we remember that we are of the natural world.

THE HEN AND THE ROOSTER

continues. . .

T HEN the King gave him water, meat, and gold,
wished him good luck. "I do not know the way to
your kingdom," confessed the King.

The prince walked a long way until he came to a tall
tree with a nest that held twelve eagle babies. He saw a
three-headed snake slithering up the trunk. Taking pity on
the eagle babies, he killed the serpent and climbed into
the nest to protect them. The grateful eaglets opened their
wings and shaded him from the harsh sun. The prince
snuggled amongst their feathers where he truly rested.

When the eagle mother returned, she offered to give
the prince a gift for his kindness. He asked to be carried
on her wings back to his world. And this she did, soaring
up between both worlds.

If memory is kept alive in order to cultivate old hatreds and resentments, it is likely to culminate in vengeance, and in a repetition of violence. But if memory is kept alive in order to transcend hateful emotions, then remembering can be healing.... There are many people who find it hard to embrace the idea of forgiveness. And it is easy to see why... Yet not to forgive means closing the door to the possibility of transformation.

—Pumla Goboo-Madikizela,
A Human Being Died That Night

Journey to Jerusalem

City of Gold

If you divide the world into them and us, and history
into ours and theirs, or if you think of history as something only you and your affiliates can possess, then
no matter what you know, no matter how noble your
intentions, you have taken one step toward the
destruction of the world.

—Robert Bringhurst, *A Tree of Meaning*

THE MORNING OF THE day of the first Arab Jewish Storytelling
Festival in Jerusalem 1994, two terrorist bombs exploded. I rushed
back from an open market in Jaffa to my hotel in Tel Aviv. The
director of the festival pulled me aside in the lobby. In an urgent
whisper she asked me not to tell the other participants about

the bombs. "They are not Jewish," she insisted. "They will want to leave. You understand how I feel." I was stunned. First, how would anyone not know that there were bombs? The atmosphere was electric with horror and the news was blaring on radio and TV in Hebrew and English in every café, street corner, shop, and lobby. Second, I thought the purpose of the festival was to come together as artists in the name of unbiased heart. Finally, did I truly side with what she said, or even understand it?

The tragedy of the situation exacerbated my already complex relationship to being in Israel. It pushed into consciousness the question about enemy and war. Why? An article by Sir Laurens van der Post that I was reading came to mind:

> This is what you must learn, to recognize your brother before the fight and not afterwards. We always recognize the brotherhood of our enemy after the fight. We must learn to recognize it before the fight.

The festival director was a child survivor from Poland. I was born after the Holocaust in a Jewish family in New York. My father's mother was from a village in Poland. Unable to conjure any reply, I touched her arm reassuringly and went to my room. "We will go to Jerusalem today," she called out. "The festival will not be canceled."

We were to attend a luncheon at the home of the President of Israel. I put on the striped silk Arabic robe I had purchased in Jaffa—clothed myself in an unworded story. I also slipped on the Tibetan ring I had purchased in Manhattan—a silver band with a mantra engraved in gold between two small corals: om mani padme hum. *The jewel in the lotus*—speaking of unconditional open heart. Reminder and protection.

However when I looked in the mirror and saw dark lines under my eyes, an uncanny rage came over me. Instantly my mind exploded with thoughts about a disappointing love affair that had driven me to change my plans and accept the invitation to represent American storytelling in Israel. Consumed with jealousy, a friend had betrayed me, caused the end of my relationship, and instigated a falling out with an organization I had worked with for ten years. I swayed under the weight of feelings of habitual defeat and unfairness. I was happy to fly to Israel, where I had lived in my early twenties until the death of my mother. And here I was confronted with danger and violence and my own discomfort.

We live in a web of remembered stories, learned beliefs, and unconscious narratives, hardly cognizant of their impact. Stories we live by, containing archetypal energy of hidden myths, influence what we do. These stories are sometimes known by us but are often deeply rooted in unconscious memory. I felt threatened, confused, sad, and enraged all at once. This feast of intense thoughts had erupted without warning. Shocked by my fury, I wept. I was also a part of the violence.

I thought about the *Bhagavad Gita*—one of the oldest spiritual discourses on the nature of reality. I sought a vaster narrative to make sense of unceasing violence, bias, betrayal, and my own catapult into vengeance and self pity. In the *Gita*, a great warrior, Prince Arjuna, was about to battle forces of evil. He was leading a huge, well weaponed army, when he suddenly recognized his opponents:

> Dejected, filled with strange pity,
> The Warrior Arjuna said to Krishna,
> "I see my kinsmen gathered here for war.
> My limbs sink, my mouth is parched.
> I see omens of chaos, Krishna;
> I see no good in killing my kinsman in battle."

During the ride to Jerusalem the conversation was about the bombing. The director was furious with us for this "indulgence." She insulted an Irish man who was asking a lot of questions about Palestinians. He was not Jewish—"How dare he compare" the pain she felt to that of Palestinians. No one argued. We all felt compassion for her and the entire situation.

We were to meet the Arab storytellers who were joining us that night. It seemed impossible that they would attend or that the festival would take place. The situation felt fraught with shock and blame. However, we arrived all together.

Once in the waiting room, set up with a long table with tea and coffee and snacks, we stood around awkwardly. No one took the initiative to make introductions. I knew that any time I had entered an Arab home, hospitality was not overlooked, regardless of circumstances. But the norms seemed to have been altered by what had occurred.

Then, President Weitzman appeared. He was gracious and eloquent. He greeted us and welcomed everyone, particularly the Arabs and the international performers, and quickly excused himself. There was no need for explanation. Moments later a door opened and we were moved into another waiting room. Chairs were arranged before a small platform. Our pre-lunch storytelling event was about to begin. I was seated beside a tall, handsome Bedouin man in a white linen suit and Arabic scarf. We smiled at one another politely.

I noticed that my good looking neighbor was staring at my ring. I lifted my hand to show it to him. Then thinking that he might like to see it more closely, I slid it off my finger. He nodded. Taking that as a further sign of interest, I pointed to the writing and handed it to him so he could see the fine detail. He looked at me for a moment and then slipped my ring onto his finger. I waited for him to give it back. He did not. He looked ahead. Then my name was called. I told a few tales very quickly and sought out my Swedish friend, who was standing at the back of the room. I had to figure out how to ask for my ring politely.

I whispered, "I don't know if I just became engaged," attempting humor. He added, "Don't ask for it. You could start a war." He also meant to be funny. I told another storyteller, who suggested that I admire the ring back. I felt ridiculous. I tried it, but nothing happened. I still wanted my ring.

Chuck Kruger, an American poet-storyteller living in Ireland, said, "A Native American gave an early settler a peace pipe. The settler hung it over his mantle. When the Indian returned the next year he was unhappy, seeing the pipe so displayed, and took it back. Gifts have to circulate or they stop being gifts. If you don't give things away they lose their spirit. Laura, you made a peace offering."

> Krishna said to Arjuna,
> "Whatever you do—what you take,
> what you offer, what you give,
> what penance you perform,
> do as an offering to me.
> I am impartial to all creatures,
> and no one is hateful or dear to me."

After lunch we were still making jokes about my "engagement"—whether I would go to live in the desert in a tent, befriend his other wives, and learn to ride a camel. I even joked about the virtues of living without rent and wearing the clothing I coveted in the market. We cavalierly engaged in wacky one liners that shaded my embarrassment and annoyance at having given my ring away.

Just as we were about to get into the van to leave, the attendant to my future husband, whom it turned out was a Bedouin prince, called to me. I walked toward him, hoping to receive back the ring. The prince smiled and held something out to me. I imagined that it was an antique brooch, or at least a priceless object that belonged to his family. He took my hand and placed something in my palm, and I watched him depart in a limousine. I opened my hand. It was a pen. Yossi Zeller, a Jewish comedian, said, "Ah it is a free pen they give out at the Bank Leumi." I felt slightly insulted. Was this equal to what I had given?

On the way to the Khan Theater, where the festival would

take place, I thought about my immediate response and Chuck's tale. While I was focused on the value of the object, perhaps the prince had focused on the value of exchange itself. I had seen another flash of my own arrogance.

We passed near the bus terminal where the bombs had exploded. It was blocked off. There were police cars. Then we drove toward the Old City. It is hard to describe the array of emotions that I felt. It was a dreamlike tapestry of disbelief and sorrow. On top of a hill at the end of a winding road I saw the city of Jerusalem: its ancient walls and the gold domed mosque. When I came to Israel in 1968, nearly twenty years earlier, there were no houses on this hill. We had driven up a dirt road. Over the years I had observed a memorial forest growing up on either side of a well tended gravel road. Now I saw a string of tall apartment buildings, made of Jerusalem's famed white and pink stone, standing alongside the well paved route to the Israeli side of the Old City. There were tourist signs for hotels and night time reenactments of the Templars, King Solomon, and The Queen of Sheba advertised.

Three religions have fought over this city. Who knows how many peoples have lived here, built here, fought here, prayed here before that? A conflagration of stories dwells here—often the same stories, but told differently or forgotten.

• • •

When I was twenty, Albert Bouwmeester, a Dutch friend, had taken me for a tour of the Church of the Rock. We visited small shrines built by different Christian faiths. We climbed to the Ethiopian church on the roof. When Albert disappeared for a half hour I was escorted by a welcoming Orthodox monk into the basement of the church. It took three times for me to notice, thinking the monk was walking too close, that he was grabbing my breast. I believed he was religious and I was imagining it. In a swift-as-a-deer leap I raced up the steps and bumped into Albert, and we fell into ripples of hilarious laughter at the incident. We went out into the stone cobbled streets, dispelling any holier-than-thou feelings we had nurtured at the start of our day's journey.

Albert had sat with me at night by the side of the Jordan River in Kibbutz Neot Mordechai, where we lived until 1969. It was above the Golan Heights and beside the mountains of Lebanon. He regaled me with stories of his guru in India, where he lived for seven years. It was the first time I had heard of anyone living with, or having, a guru. After my "religious incident" we celebrated the zaniness of life in a small Armenian restaurant and walked safely after dark, purchasing embroidered scarves, small quilted camel blankets, and tiny painted glasses in the Old City, which had just opened up to Jews and tourists after the Six Day War.

• • •

Instead of dinner, that evening Chuck and I took a walk into the Old City to make prayers at the Wailing Wall before our festival performance. We separated at the men's and women's sides of the wall to tuck prayers on small papers into cracks between the stones and wish for peace. A woman said to me, "I see you want to begin your life over. It is good to go to the holy city of Jerusalem at that time."

A few hours later in the theater, the Arab tellers did not want to begin the evening and the Israelis said they did not want to either. I agreed to, saying I was Jewish but loved Arabic stories. I told the story that my friend and mentor Jean Sviadac had told me in Paris en route to Israel:

> Nasruddin was the judge in a small village where three families had killed each other for generations. The judge asked the oldest man in each family to tell his side of the story. Each man spoke, saying his version was true, ending his story with the words, "He is wrong. I am right." They waited for the judge to make his decision. After listening, Nasruddin said, "What's the problem if you are all right?"

The Bedouin prince was standing at the back of the room. He was enjoying the story, which he may have known. He had his attendant bring tea and cakes onto the stage for me when I finished. I told a second Nasruddin tale:

> Can there be peace in the world? Perhaps. Once Nasruddin was pouring milk into a river. "What are you doing?" asked a passerby. "I'm making yogurt," answered Nasruddin. "That's impossible," said the man. Nasruddin replied, "But what if it works?"

My almost husband clapped loudly again. I took the white linen napkin that sat under the tea he had sent up earlier and, with the Leumi pen he had given me, I wrote THANK YOU in big letters. I hoped he appreciated the use of his gift for this message.

> Krishna said to Arjuna,
> "When one knows the self to be
> indestructible, enduring, unborn, unchanging,
> how does he kill or cause anyone to kill?"

In Tel Aviv at the hotel that night I was awakened by the howling of a dog. I was sure he was being beaten by a man in a nearby house. The dog's cries of pain were soon interrupted by a fierce growling. I went downstairs to the lobby of the hotel in my nightgown. "We have to save the dog," I begged. The hotel clerk said, "Listen, lady, why don't you shut your window, then you won't hear it." I went outside, but the dog's barking had stopped. Did I make it up? Was that my own story coloring my ears? I went back to my room and gave up on sleep. I tried to phone the man in England whom I had hoped to visit before our break up. I rang his phone again and again and there was no answer.

My heartbeats quieted as I looked at Krishna through the eyes of Arjuna, as Krishna showed him his omnipresent wrathful form.

Arjuna said,
"Tell me who you are
in this terrible form?
I do not understand
the course of your ways."

Krishna talked about those caught in the snare of desire—
those who say, "I have killed that enemy and I shall kill others.
I am the lord, I am the enjoyer, successful, strong and happy."
He described them as those who hate and revile him and fall
"into a demonic womb deluded in birth after birth."

"Arjuna, when a fool cannot escape
dreaming, fear, grief, depression, and
intoxication, courage is darkly inert.

"Arjuna, now hear about joy,
the three ways of finding delight
through practice that
brings an end to suffering."

Sanjay, the ancient poet who recorded the story of the *Bhagavad
Gita*, ended it:

Where Krishna is lord of discipline and Arjuna is the archer,
there do fortune, abundance, and morality exist.

Recollecting this story I found solace, beyond solution. I wondered if I could risk cheering up in the middle of my own desire,
obsession, confusion, and grief. In listening, the mind rests in
experience between explanation and bias, reaching into the
chasms of unconditional unbiased mind, and for an instant the
endless web of right and wrong seems useless.

Nonetheless, I made a plan to leave Israel and attempt to
"find" the lover who had abandoned me and find out the truth

about what had happened. At the airport, I changed my flight. I realized I could let go of the imagined end to my story, but lacked the strength. I spent two terrible days attempting to reach him. At the end of that time we met. He explained his side of the story, or at least what he wanted to reveal. I was mortified and finally wept again, losing a night of sleep.

In the early morning I walked in the rain on Portobello Road, trying to find a cappuccino without waking my host or her family. By coincidence, I happened upon an old friend who was opening an Afghan rug shop several hours early. He saw my tears, sat me down on a pile of rugs, and went to find the life-saving cappuccino. When he returned I told him my entire story: the end of the love affair, the bombings in Israel, my mother's death, and the final conversation. As he listened, I was astonished by his kindness. I thought, "This is what I need—a man whose weapon is gentleness, who knows the balm of listening without fixing." I exhausted myself in the telling and closed my eyes.

Meanwhile, my friend stood up. I opened my eyes to see him standing above me, arms raised in rage. He roared like a demon, "You are my sister. I will kill him for lying to you." I believed him. In his empty hand I saw a sword and on his face a mask of violence that was terrifying. Suddenly, I found myself begging him to do nothing—not to risk going to jail. I was asking him to save the life of the one who had betrayed me. For a moment we both grew silent and then began to laugh. I told him about the pen. He pressed a carnelian and silver ring into the palm of my hand.

Reflection

I am intrigued by this fragment from a long poem about an Inuit woman telling a story to her husband. How little I know about the actual magic of language and the living power of imagination.

> One day the man came home from his qalgi [ceremonial
>   house],
> and when he got home, he asked his wife to tell a story:
>
> When she finally gave in, she said,
> "I will tell a story. But you must keep it secret.
> I will tell an unipkaaq [old story]."
> ...She said, "Listen! And I'll tell you my unipkaaq."
>
> The woman put her arm in the katak [entrance hole]
>   and stirred in a circle.
> "Don't be scared when things start to happen," she said,
> "You asked for an unipkaaq!"
> Now as the woman stirred, they heard splashing.
> It came from the katak,
> And the entrance passage started filling with water.
> The man saw water rising in the iglu.
> Then the katak flooded.
> ...then something burst, and a whale appeared.
> A whale rose in the katak, blocking the entrance.
> It spouted in the katak.
>
> "Since you'll keep this a secret, we can eat some," said
>   the woman.
> They ate part of it.

—Tom Lowenstein,
Ancient Land, Sacred Whale

A story is never random. It must be framed with fierce attention, trust and affection. Telling a story is always an act of faith. Whenever order is broken, chaos is unleashed. Story is a sacred visualization. There are lessons along the way.

—Terry Tempest Williams,
Pieces of White Shell

Sudden Story

$\mathcal{T}$ HREE TIMES IN TWO years, a story-to-tell came to me with sudden and irresistible force in a challenging situation. Having no choice but to respond to its call, I discovered each tale to be the touchstone of grace and meaning for my troubled audience. What made it the "right story" had as much or more to do with the nature of listening itself as the literal content of the tale alone.

I was invited to tell stories to three small groups of junior high school students in Chinatown, New York, who were involved in violent racial conflicts. The teachers approved of my proposal to spend five days in the school, though the principal was not convinced of the value of storytelling. He asked me to meet him and discuss the exact plan, and expected results from the five days. During the meeting, I explained that I would not speak to the students directly of the conflict or make any judgments of their behavior. My plan was simply to tell a mix of stories, from traditional folktales to my own personal narratives. I was unsure of the outcome. The storytelling might continue for all five days or, based on their response, I might work to develop some kind of dialogue and storytelling among the kids themselves.

My true goal was to place them together in a room where listening was the intention. I told the principal that the effect of such intentional story-listening is a synchronization of mind and body as each person creatively reconstructs the story being told through their own imaginative response. Violence, whether racially motivated or otherwise, occurs as a reaction when one is out of the body. The perpetrators have no sense of self or other. Listening to a storyteller, the young people are emotionally, viscerally, and intelligently engaged in the story, which naturally stimulates a mind/body synchronicity in the listening. In other words, as they fall under the spell of the story that they are recreating in their mind's eye, they simultaneously fall into their own bodies. Drawn out of self-involved projections and concerns, they fall wholeheartedly into becoming all sides of the story event.

Touched by what I said, albeit a bit wary, the principal agreed.

My first day I went to all three classrooms. In each I told "The Necklace," (included in an earlier chapter of this book); a personal tale about an encounter with a gang of boys on 8th Street; and the Moroccan tale of "The Wild Girl," (from, respectively, my recordings *Moon On Fire,* Yellow Moon Press; *Making Peace,* Earwig Music; *Nightwalkers,* Yellow Moon Press). At the end of the three tales, I asked if anyone had any questions or thoughts about the stories. The first group sat quietly at first, until five of the six kids asked if they could come with me to the second classroom. Their teacher agreed. In the second room, a Chinese boy raised his hand after the question and said, "I know that story ("The Wild Girl") is true because my mother had to sell her gold bracelets for rice when she was running away from home during the revolution." Everyone's eyes turned toward him. One of the

African American girls blurted out, "That is bad. I didn't know that."

Creating a council (based on the work of Jack Zimmerman, *The Way of Council*, Bramble Books), I asked, "Is there any situation that you are ever in where you have to do something you really don't want to do to survive?" I was referring to "The Necklace," where a girl agrees to lick the open sores of a monster-hag to retrieve what she has lost. A tall girl, her legs thrust out into the aisle in a defiant manner, pulled in her legs, sat up, and said, "Every morning I have to wash, dress, and feed my eleven-year-old retarded brother. Then after school, I have to babysit him and he has to come with me. Then, I have to put him to bed. Man, I never get time to do my homework." I understood why she fell asleep during the day, one of her teacher's main complaints about her behavior. It went on like that.

The next day I told a long fairytale and managed to have the entire three groups with me for all sessions. We talked about what we would dream of being if we could do anything in the world. The same tall girl, whom I was also told picks fights with kids, said, "I would be a nurse because I have a lot of patience." We all laughed in agreement. A boy known for his anger said he wanted to be a veterinarian. The teacher was amazed. The kids were completely intrigued by each other. I set up a council on the other days where they each sat around and spoke about their home lives. They had no idea about each other and were astonished to learn about each other's lives: their difficulties, their situations, their histories, their victories, the languages their parents spoke at home, etc.

The poet Rumi writes, "The branches of your intelligence grow new leaves in the wind of this listening. The body reaches a peace. Rooster sound comes, reminding you of your love for dawn."[18] As the children heard my stories, their bodies could reach the peace that anchors deep listening. In this state of peace, a new awareness of each other—the "rooster sound" of dawn— becomes possible. Watching their faces, I saw their masks of apathy melt and their true interest in each other emerge. They each had basic goodness and intelligence, which was uncovered and activated during the telling, no matter what their personal history was. The dynamic listening engendered through the telling is an exercise in personal and internal peacekeeping. The process of listening is a natural process of resting the mind, enabling it "to grow new leaves."

. . .

Another "sudden" storytelling took place in an elementary school. There had been a murder in the schoolyard. The staff asked if I could come to the school in the afternoon, after lunch hour, and tell stories for an hour while an emergency meeting was held for all the teachers and staff. Without thinking, carried by the urgency of the request, I agreed.

When I arrived in the auditorium I regretted my decision. The entire school was gathered, from first grade to fifth grade. They were in a state of extreme agitation, supervised only by a music teacher on the stage attempting to get them to sing. Half were singing and half were jumping around, squeaking the chairs, or hitting one another. The teacher was delighted to see me and quickly leapt off the stage to move me onto it. I was announced, but no one seemed to hear. A few looked at me, but most continued what they were doing. I had planned an hour of shorter, pithy, entertaining tales, but now, seeing the situation, I had no idea what to do.

Suddenly, a long fairytale came to mind. It was about a young prince who is able—through his innocent fearlessness and kindness—to wound a monster who was responsible for destroying peace. The prince's journey was through three descending worlds. In each world there was another monster to overcome; the root causes had to be found beneath the obvious problems. His inherent kindness was made conscious and he became a true ruler, of himself and his world.

It is a long story, fraught with adventure. It secretly describes a very unrelenting and important psychological journey of healing. I have to admit I was not thinking of this at the moment the story came to me. But since no one was paying attention to me, and I could not responsibly leave the room, being the only adult present, I whispered into the microphone with intensity what seemed most honest at the moment: "I have been asked to come here and tell you a story. I know you don't seem to be listening, however, I have to stay for the hour. I am going to tell you my favorite story. It is a fairytale. It is filled with monsters and blood and adventures, heroes and heroines, and I am going to tell it anyway whether you listen or not." The noise continued.

I began, "There was once a king and a queen who had two treasures..."

Suddenly, the students began to listen. I told the story as if my life depended on it. I felt as if I were holding every single one of them in the palm of my hand. I entered the story as whole-heartedly as the children. As the storyteller, the story's landscape arose between us. When I was the characters, the landscape surrounded me. The listeners followed this shifting imaginary perspective, expanding their minds as the story unfolded, sharing with me a living, pulsating dream. They laughed and were silent; they cried out in response if I asked a question, and listened carefully to find out what was going to happen next. I was amazed at the whole thing. I felt my being was a center tent pole that held up the canvas of our reciprocal event. Their attention nurtured me and my attention focused them.

When it was over they were quiet for a moment. I thanked them and asked if they had any questions, since the staff meeting was still going on. A girl raised her hand and asked if I knew Aladdin. I was confused. A boy said, "Yeah. Aladdin and his magic lamp. You must know Aladdin." It was their knowledge of myth and fairytale through Disney films. I said of course I knew about Aladdin and that the tale I told might also have been told as one of the 1001 tales told by a storyteller named Scheherazade. I then told them about her, and how she transformed the wicked heart of a ruthless king by telling him stories. "Far out." "That is cool." "Michael Jordan would like this!" they commented.

Then the music teacher returned and began to yell at them to line up. She was strident, worried, demanding, and screaming. I got off the stage, and their reaction to such shouting was to begin shouting and pushing again. I could barely get out of the auditorium. But each time a child saw me, they said, calmly, "Thanks. That was a good story." The music teacher grabbed me by the arm, frustrated, and said, "Maybe I should have become a storyteller." If I had had time I might have explained that the story was secondary to my willingness not to blame them or attack them for a situation that was frightening and out of their control. I had attempted to meet and engage their energy. The music teacher herself was out of her body, hoping the children would control themselves while she was unable to contain her own fears and frustrations. Her words of control were heard by the children as expressions of her own lack of it.

. . .

The last emergency telling was the most demanding for me. I was in a taxi with a fifteen-year-old boy, Alusine Bah, an ex-child soldier from Sierra Leone, who had to return to the war. He had been brought to the United Nations in New York (along with my son, Ishmael Beah) to speak on behalf of children forced into involvement in war. He had been safe for ten days. Now he was sobbing in the taxi. I had been convinced by the organization I worked for that I could not keep him illegally in New York, which is what he'd hoped I would do. "No other child may ever get a visa to get out," they explained. I felt like I was taking him to the slaughterhouse. I did not know what to do or say to him. Finally, I said, "What can I do for you? I am so sorry. I wish I could keep you here with me. I will not forget you for a single day. You will live in my heart every minute."

He said, "Please, tell me a story."

I was so completely anxious that I did not know what story to tell. Then, as with the other emergencies, a story came to mind and it was the only one that came to mind. So, to the great surprise of the relief worker who shared our taxi, I told it. "There was once a poor boy who went to a market. He had no money to buy anything. He wanted everything. In the market was a magician performing a magic act. He had a magic finger. Anything he touched turned to gold. The boy watched the magician with amazement. The magician asked, 'Would you like some gold?'[19]

"The boy said, 'Yes.'

"The magician turned a mouse to gold. But the boy refused it. He said, 'I want more.' "The magician turned one thing after another to gold, each thing larger than the last. The boy continued to reject his offers, saying, 'I want more.' At last the magician demanded, 'What do you want?'

"The boy answered, 'I want a magic finger.'"

As I told it the boy was listening. His heart slowed down and his hysteria diminished. I held his hand as I spoke, feeling not up to the hugeness of his pain. Puzzled, the humanitarian worker in the taxi said, "What good was that story?" But the boy said, "I understood the story. The boy will survive because he will settle for nothing less than his future."

I was amazed now. He leaned back into my arms and cried quietly. I wept with him as did the other woman. Months and months later, after I lost touch with him and feared he was dead because the war had erupted in all its virulence, he finally was able to call me again. I promised to phone him every Friday morning at a public phone in Freetown. It was one of three phones in the city that were working. I called for one year. Sometimes he called me weeping and frustrated. He was agitated by terror and hopelessness.

What do you say to a child who is in the middle of a war, a boy who knows that any minute he can be killed? Who knows that food is scarce and justice is not real? I thought about the story and our communication in the taxi. We spoke each time about staying rooted in his body and not giving way to hysteria no matter what happened. With awareness he could keep hold of his mind and know what to do. With hysteria and retraumatization he would go mad and lose the ability to make immediate decisions. I kept asking him if he knew the difference between losing his grip and becoming traumatized, and when he could feel his feelings and stay alert. He said he knew. We talked about this: about how to bring his mind back. About how to put his head down on his knees (if possible) the moment he felt himself falling into terror and then looking at what was around him and not getting carried away with reactivity. We talked about how that sense of staying aware in the midst of chaos was his magic finger.

Eventually I had the pleasure of helping to bring him out of Sierra Leone into Ghana, where he was finally out of war's way. When we talk now, fifteen years later, we remind each other of the truth of our shared story, and the lesson of holding one's mind in the midst of chaos. Alusine is a college graduate working on behalf of children affected by wars.

. . .

I realized much later that these sudden stories were only possible because two abiding foundations support my work and life. The first is that I know many stories and have thought much about their inner meanings and how the response of each listener fulfills the potential riches that the text engenders. The second is that I, like the children, enjoy listening, and respect the effect of the storytelling itself more than any explicit moral that might be learned or abstracted from the story.

The story experience as a whole is the teaching and the meaning; and trusting the experience of the listener during the story creates an unforgettable knowing. The listeners are the stage on which the story erupts and resolves. A spoken or pointed-out moral teaching conceived and added to the end of a tale dilutes the listener's potent experience of becoming one with the story—

becoming both the cause and the effect of the problem in the story. Becoming the good and the bad characters helps the listener gain an inner experience of the cause and effect of actions on self, other, and the natural world. The spontaneous involvement in an unfolding story stimulates the creation of an inner story regardless of whether one recalls a specific lesson later. Living the reenactment of the event makes each child aware within themselves of those parts that are capable of both good and evil. Participating in the event of storytelling itself conjures an oasis of communion with others as well as a direct access for mental stability.

The poet Rumi says, "There's a moon inside every human being. Learn to be companions with it. Give more of your life to this listening."

The boy from Sierra Leone, the children in a school where a murder had taken place, the students fighting over race—how can a storyteller remember the moon that reflects light in the midst of their individual and collective darkness? My stories could only be released when, as Rumi reminds us, I tried to be a companion to what was hidden in them, to give my own life to this listening. In emergency tellings like this, the content of the story is the outer garment only. The story alone taken literally does nothing to change, transform, or move the mind and heart into another way of perceiving. It is the living, reciprocal sharing that opens deeper into another level of meaning that is far more significant.

It is easy to forget how mysterious and mighty stories are. They do their work with all the internal materials of the mind and self. They become part of you while changing you. Beware the stories you read or tell: subtly, at night, beneath the waters of consciousness, they are altering your world.

—BEN OKRI, *Birds of Heaven*

THE HEN AND THE ROOSTER

The prince continued his search...

...for the maiden with the hen and the rooster. He traveled until at last he found himself returned to the place where the bald-headed lute player had carried the maiden down into the earth. She was there.

He asked, "Where is the bald-headed lute player?

She answered, "The moment that he carried me away, he fell asleep. He has been asleep for three years."

"How can I destroy him and take you as my bride?"

"It is not necessary to destroy him," she said. "There is a cage with nine locks. Inside are three birds. One is his strength, one is his heart, and one is his spirit. If you open the nine locks and set the birds free, the lute player will awaken. His heart, his soul, and his strength will return to his body and he will do no more harm."

In the end, it may be for want of myths that we perish, and only through courage to live them that we become truly whole.

MARC IAN BARASCH, HEALING DREAMS

Deadly Play

$\mathcal{I}$N A POOR COUNTRY devastated by nine years of civil war, a guerrilla army was conducting a campaign of death and mutilation so unrelenting it was called "No Living Thing." Thousands of those conscripted to carry out this violence were children. This was a hell on earth, a place where a young girl, hands cut off at the wrist and tied to her waist by another child, was sent walking as a living billboard advertising the end of hope and compassion. It was a place of deadly play.

I once taught drama in the converted ballroom of a private Catholic elementary school in New York. The children's favorite game was an ongoing battle between the forces of Good and Evil. The Good were led by a magic Wizard, the Evil were led by a wicked General, and the children shifted allegiances readily, exploring both sides. They savored conducting merciless attacks on one another and constructing make-believe torture rooms.

The highlight of play occurred when someone from either side was killed. The children made a circle and, under the direction of the Wizard, sang the dead children back to life. Then the battle continued. New episodes were invented until the bell that marked the end of the class. Exhausted and happy, the children gathered to retell their adventures before leaving for math, religion, or history.

Not one of these children, or I, could have imagined that at the same time thousands of children of the same age, armed with guns and machetes, were being sent into real battles to kill and be killed, with no one to sing them back to life.

"No Living Thing" was the motto of rebel forces in Sierra Leone, West Africa. Eighty percent of the guerrillas were thought to be children between the ages of five and seventeen. Born into violence, raised as killers, they were trained to commit mutilation and murder. Like all children, they learned by example: adults forced them to witness atrocities before taking them to neighboring villages to do it themselves.

This situation was unique only in its brutality. The use of children as soldiers is on the increase in many parts of the world. The United Nations estimates the number of child soldiers globally at more than 300,000. At the same time, the age of the children is decreasing: children as young as four are seen using the weapons of war.

The statistics: 10 percent of an estimated 60,000 combatants in Liberia may have be children; at least 20 percent in El Salvador; 10 percent in Afghanistan. Nearly 70 percent of Palestinian children are believed to have participated in acts of political violence. And so on.

The justifications: Children make the best soldiers because they carry out orders without question. Having lost families and suffering from trauma, they find security in the army. Small children, knowing nothing other than violence, will fight until they die. They make better spies and messengers because of their size. They do not ask for salaries. Children can be used as human shields or sent ahead of armies to test for landmines.

UNICEF concludes that the proliferation of child soldiers also arises from the ease of using light and devastating weapons. The AK 47 can be stripped and reassembled by a child of ten.

In her groundbreaking 1996 U.N. report, Graca Michel wrote, "More and more of the world is being sucked into a desolate moral vacuum. This is a space devoid of the most basic human values; a space in which children are slaughtered, raped, and maimed; a space in which children are exploited as soldiers.... There are few further depths to which humanity can sink."

In the fall of 1996 I worked as a facilitator for "Children's Voices," a UNICEF conference at the United Nations at which children from twenty-three countries spoke. There I met an orphaned former child soldier from West Africa named Ishmael. At the time, he was fifteen years old. He wrote songs about peace and longed for an education. I stayed in close contact with him afterwards and, after a long and difficult process, brought him to this country to build a new life. Here is some of his story.[20]

"When I was eleven years old my parents and brothers were killed in the civil war. I hid for eight months. Often alone, living in trees in the bush, hardly eating, I suffered from malnutrition. I was told that if I joined the forces I could have food, and take revenge for the death of my family. I was also told that if I did not become a soldier I would be killed.

"I had no choice. I became a soldier. I learned to shoot a gun. That was my training. Then I was sent into my first battle. All around me people were dying. In front of me people were dying. I could not imagine killing a human being, but a grown man kept shouting at me, 'Shoot! Shoot!' Then I shot. I killed for the first time. And I was no longer of this world."

I asked him what he lost in those years of being a soldier, besides the obvious losses of family and home. He answered, "I lost my self in the war, my self, my image, my sense of feeling for myself and other children. I lost my ability to think before doing. I just kept going.

"That's what happens to every child soldier. Children are the best soldiers because they can be used to do whatever you ask them to do. The grown-ups give you drugs and torture you. The littlest children usually get killed. They have no maturity. Their minds are all mixed up and they will never give up until they die. They think that the only way to live is to fight.

"When the war broke out everyone became stupid and did not think. Because of guns and trauma and drugs you cannot think. Adults need to raise their children with the idea of forgiveness, not revenge. Otherwise it will never stop."

I asked him how he was able to leave the army. He explained that the children were never left alone, so that they had no chance to think. "Once I was in the bush alone. I do not know where it came from, but I had a thought that I was no longer a good boy. Then it went away."

Later, when there were no battles, U.N. workers came looking for child soldiers to encourage them to undergo detraumatization. "I was not normal. I was crazy. I did not want to stop fighting. But I recognized one of the men. He was from my village. He saw me. When he recognized me he said, 'Oh my God!' His face was very sad. I realized I was no longer a good child. 'What am I doing?' I asked myself. It was later that I went for detraumatization. It was very hard. It was very painful to become a normal human being again, because I had to feel, remember, and dream again.

"Some child soldiers in the future will change. But it will take a long time. It is hard to find people who really care about us and are willing to work with us. We were not normal. These children who do not get help will end up in a bad situation because they do not think before they act. So you see, in the future there will be more trouble."

What story in the world best describes the atrocity of turning children into killers? What story offers some clues of redemption, or understanding of this awful wound in the psyche of the world? Perhaps it is the wild destruction unleashed by Dionysus, god of ecstasy and the vine.

Dionysus, twice-born child, wearing two masks, reveals the darkest possibilities of human nature—and the most joyous. At the height of his murderous frenzy arises the birth of song; a natural stream of light evolves from the unrelenting darkness of murder and death.

Thinking about his cult, I have sought some medicine for the depravity of turning children into soldiers in the world today. Knowing such darkness, can they become protectors of peace and compassion? Knowing about them, can we face our own shadows and liberate kindness without judgment? Can we find a place for these children in our world?

A country like Sierra Leone, whose unnatural borders were created by colonial powers that disregarded tribal traditions and hierarchies, was once infused by rituals and myths that included awareness of both the dark and the light. Tremendous energy went into rites of passage that brought children into contact with the realms of ancestors, spirits, and demons, both good and bad.

But colonial powers ignored this process of rebalancing life and devalued the transmutation of dark forces within and without. Where did the suppressed shadows go? Perhaps, not acknowledged or contained by myth and ritual, these dark forces arose as the displays of evil and destruction that plague Africa today.

At the U.N. conference, the boy was given five minutes to speak about the children of his country. Ishmael brought the room to silence.

"I joined the forces because of the loss of my parents, and hunger. It is not easy to be a soldier, but we just had to do it." Putting down his paper, he looked around and smiled shyly. "I am reintegrated. You don't have to be afraid of me. I am not a soldier anymore. Now I am a child. We are all brothers and sisters."

Sitting straight, radiating dignity, he continued: "This is what I have learned and want to say: revenge is not good. I killed to revenge the death of my parents. But if I continue to revenge, if another is killed and then another, then there will only be more revenge and it will never come to an end."

Following the children's presentations, a journalist asked a girl from Albania: "What are the causes of war?" She answered gently, "We are more interested in what are the causes of peace."

According to a folk tale from Zimbabwe told to me by Ephat Mujuru, the origin of murder was the death of a child.

A mother left her baby beneath a tree while she worked in the field. When it cried, a large eagle landed on the basket holding the child. The bird comforted the baby, and it stopped crying. Every day when the baby cried, the eagle comforted it.

When the mother told her husband, he did not believe her. He went out to the field. The eagle flew to the crying baby. The husband grew afraid. He lifted his bow and shot at the bird. The eagle flew away, but the baby was killed. That was the first murder. Since that time people have killed each other.

The man did not trust the word of the mother; he did not trust the natural world. I told this story to Ishmael. He said softly, "No one thinks. In their mind they know they are doing something wrong, but few people want to stop or apologize. Some people do not listen to their mind. They are too proud to feel."

He described the painful process of detraumatization as a coming back to this world, a harrowing reawakening of feeling, thinking, sensing, and remembering.

One day walking uptown from our home on Broadway, Ishmael said, "You know, in war all of nature is lost. You cannot hear the sounds of the bush or the birds. You only hear gunshots. When you walk through empty villages it is so sad. No birds sing. Even the buildings begin to collapse without human warmth or the sounds of nature. It is a terrible silence."

In her U.N. report, Graca Michal called for an immediate, global demobilization of child soldiers. She asked all armies to create "peace zones" for children. In a personal note at the end of her presentation, she added, "Above all else, this process has strengthened my conviction that we must do anything and everything to protect children, to give them priority and a better future. This is a call to embrace a new morality that places children where they belong—at the heart of all agendas. Ask yourselves what you can do to make a difference. Then take action, no matter how large or how small, for our children have a right to peace."

The stories people tell have a way of taking care of them. If stories come to you, care for them. And learn to give them away where they are needed. Sometimes a person needs a story more than food to stay alive. That is why we put these stories in each other's memories.

—BARRY LOPEZ, *Crow and Weasel*

Strong Medicine

A strong disease needs a strong medicine.

—Mende proverb, Sierra Leone

HEARING ABOUT WHAT OCCURRED during the civil war in
Sierra Leone from the lips of children forced to kill or be killed,
those whose arms and legs were cut with blunt machetes, or
those designated as "bush wives" for grown men, changed my
life in 1996. Coming to know the resilience, gentleness, and generosity of these children made a greater impact.

The first afternoon of the Young Voices Conference each of
the children told their stories. Alusine and Ishmael stood together,
weeping, their faces contorted, to reveal a misery and violence
that was hard to reconcile with the sweetness of their voices. I
had no place in my own experience to contain the harshness of

what they had lived through. Their tragedies, along with those of the others, incanted hour after hour, brought up memories of the Holocaust and of what I had seen only in films and newscasts. For each of the fifty-seven children, it was a small miracle to be together and to be heard. Some of them had risked their lives to be there. The way they shared their narratives was a lesson in itself. A quality of "joy to be alive" framed the tellings, and the tellings seemed to be generous, without self-reference, although they were so deeply personal. They were giving voice for all the children who are forced into unasked-for chaos, poverty, and violence.

I was hired to spend two hours a day at the conference. However, the choice-less decision to bear witness daily inspired my every morning's walk to UNICEF and my every late-night bus ride home. My constant thought was, "What if someone had flown me out of the Holocaust fifty years ago to speak about my trauma, and then flew me back?"

Several years later, when I brought Ishmael out of Sierra Leone to New York, I learned that he had been astonished when I introduced myself as a storyteller. On one of our first mornings as mother and son, he shared with me that while visiting his grandmother during the harvest season in Mattru Jong, he sat every evening in a circle with villagers and listened to stories. He could never forget the feeling, although he sadly admitted he could barely remember the tales. Ishmael explained how important it was for each child to be able to re-tell the story correctly. The result of this, he began to recognize, was strengthening heightened awareness and listening skills, as well as making everyone a part of a long history still unfolding.

So I asked Ishmael for any story he remembered. This is the fragment he told me. Later, Ishmael recalled the entire story and the storyteller, named Lele Gombe, "who knew how to make a story come alive so it was not forgotten." The more Ishmael healed, the more he recalled.

"There was one story. Yes, I wish I could remember it. It is about a man who washed himself every morning. He took out each organ, cleaned it, and replaced it. One day he took out his heart but forgot to put it back in his body. He was a nice man, but when he went out that day without his heart he insulted everyone he met. He ignored old people and those in need. He had so many arguments that everyone asked him what was the problem. Then he remembered that he had not put back his heart. He went home. It was still on the table. He put his heart back in his body. He went out and said he was sorry to everyone."

• • •

At the end of 2007, Ishmael and I traveled to Montreal, where Alusine was living. They were both receiving Canadian Peace Awards. For the first time since that day in 1996, Alusine, encouraged by my son's book *A Long Way Gone*, told his story publicly. At the Montreal YMCA, there was not a dry eye in the room. His voice was strong because he told his tale without shame, with feeling and vivid details. He told his life story, just as Ishmael has, from the point of view of the one who has experienced the horror and come through it with sanity and dignity intact. It was the time for his own medicine to be stimulated. It was the moment he could reveal the story beyond a litany of events. He spoke as someone who is scarred with unbearable memory but does not drown in the misery. I was relieved to know that he was not being asked to speak to sensationalize his story for others or to feel sorry for himself.

Since that first meeting twelve years ago, both of these young men have taught me the true role of the storyteller, the genuine listener/hearer, and the power of story. These boys, who had lived through the devastating chaos and inhumanity of war, had grown up listening to stories. They each had the innate capacity to speak from their hearts and to discern the heart of a tale.

In 1996, unable to keep them in New York, I promised to help both boys if I could. Then in 1998, after a long, frustrating journey through two African countries where Ishmael's visa was denied, I managed to speak to the then-ambassador of a third country. By drawing on my storytelling skills, making my plea with urgency, I managed to penetrate his bureaucratic mindset. At the end of my tale I asked him, "What if this boy is the next Martin Luther King or the next Nelson Mandela, and you did not sign the visa?" He signed the visa and said, "I am not sure why I am doing this. I could lose my job. Let me know what happens." Ishmael arrived in New York City soon after. It was another four years before Alusine traveled to Canada. His story was different.

I hardly remembered how Ishmael looked as I waited for him at the airport. Nearly two years had passed. The conference haunted me with the ephemeral vividness of a dream. The day before he boarded his flight to the U.S., I told him that he could travel with me all summer and rest, but when it was time for him to begin school in the fall I would find a "real" family for him. There was a silence that could cut diamonds. He responded, "I thought you were going to be my mother." The thought entered my mind stream, "What kind of a human being are you?" In an instant, I felt every cell in my body adjust with an inexplicable sensation of binding decision. "You are right," I said. "I am your mother." That was that, as fast and decisive as an event in a fairy-tale, and as true as the best of stories.

The first night Ishmael slept in his own room. "Where do you sleep?" he asked. I showed him my room and explained how in the U.S. we all sleep in separate rooms and beds. Everything we encountered together was new territory for both of us. I awkwardly tucked him in and said goodnight. My own being in my story was demanding that I have no preconceptions; however, my story of being a mother to an adolescent boy from Africa was awkward.

He shyly called to me as I started to leave the bedroom, "Hey, I imagined you would tell me a story."

I went back. I sat on the bed and placed my hand on his forehead. He said, "It is so long since I felt a mother's touch."

After all the years of storytelling on stages, confident and easily deciding what story to tell, when and to whom, now I drew a blank. Then, out of the blue, a story came to mind. Although I reflected that it was not exactly a bedtime tale for a new son, I told it.

It was one of the first stories I'd ever told. I recorded it with music by Steve Gorn, with a chant I invented based on what I thought were the right sounds. The story came from a book that I had found in a school years before, published by the Board of Education in the 1930s. The book compiled African folk tales with no sources, no countries or tribes. I read the story, loved it, and told it, unaware of protocols and copyrights at the time. When I went back to the school a year later the book was gone, along with all the old precious folktale books published in the years before 1940.

The tale I told that night was about two brothers who loved to walk. They traveled all the way to a distant village and were told by the chief that they could eat and sleep in the village, but if they snored in the village they would lose their heads. Of course they ate and fell asleep, and one of the brothers began to snore. I was hardly into the story when Ishmael began to sing. I stopped speaking to listen.

"I know this story," he said in amazement. "It is a Mende tale." (Ishmael's family tribe is Mende.) I heard it when I was growing up. This is the song." He continued to sing and then I finished the story about how the two brothers saved their lives with the song.

Ishmael and I began walking and talking daily, and while doing so, shared stories about our lives. How else would we come to know one another across the gap of cultures, the tragedies, and the strangeness of our new relationship? During one of those walks, Ishmael told me how singing a rap song had saved his life.

I reminded him of the songs he sang at the U.N. that a friend and I recorded, and how, through those hours of recordings, I came to know and trust him by the sound of his voice. That is how he came to be chosen to attend the conference at the U.N. Song, story, sharing something far bigger than himself. The words were of war; the voice was from the heart.

That summer we did travel together. To Ishmael's amazement, we went to storytelling festivals. I had no idea of the healing nature of that journey. I avoided asking about his life during the war and began to ask about his childhood before. He rented bikes wherever we went. He bicycled knowing he was safe. We ate new foods and laughed a lot.

In dealing with extreme situations of suffering, conventional thought tells us that sharing one's traumatizing experiences begins to bring someone home to his or her capacity to survive. What we discovered was that by not focusing on that story during those first years, we strengthened Ishmael's inner narrative of a place and a time before the trauma. We focused on his building a life as a normal person with friends and school and a home. Then, later, when his inner joy was rediscovered and intact, he began revisiting the painful story. This process protected him from re-traumatizing himself or deluding himself with the idea that just telling it a few times and shedding tears would provide him the sanity to live with the deep memory of a time unspeakably printed in his mind and heart forever.

As time passed, we both began to understand the immense power of having grown up with cultural oral tales shared over and over, never printed or edited, but spoken and discussed, learned, reflected on. These living tales offered templates for inner meaning and morality. The idea of punishment and reward as the inspiration for listening and participating in community was frail compared to the untarnished inner responsibility and compassion engendered through the stories and the telling situation that was unforgettable. The listener/teller became the owner of that which could turn everything to gold.

THE HEN AND THE ROOSTER
And then...

...The prince broke open the nine locks and set the birds free.

The bald-headed lute player awoke. Nothing more of him is known but that he did no more harm. His music still exists and can be heard by those with the ears to listen.

As for the prince, he and the maiden returned to his father's kingdom with the rooster and the hen. Just as they placed the birds on top of the tower of the holy temple he had built, the same old man passed by and said, "Now there is no fault within or without."

The aging king entered the building. He placed the crown on his son's head. He placed another crown on the maiden's head and she and the prince were wed. It said that they lived and ruled together with great kindness and wisdom. Because of that there was peace in the world for a long time.

A story does many things. It entertains, it informs, it instructs. It is the most complete way of communicating. If you look at these stories carefully you will find that they support and reinforce the basic tenets of a culture. The storytellers worked out what is right and wrong, what is courageous and what is cowardly, and they translated that into stories.

CHINUA ACHEBE

Monkey Mind

ONE EVENING I TOLD Ishmael a story that I had read, from the Lemba tribe of Sierra Leone. One of the cheerful memories of his early life had been the recalling of stories that he was told in his grandmother's village as a child.

The story that I read was a difficult and complicated tale about a mother and a son. It was about forgetting interdependence and about forgiving; about the reality of the spirit of the natural world; and how when things go out of balance a new balance has to be made. In the tale was the possible death of the son inadvertently caused by the mother and her ultimate death. It was also about a way of seeing that expanded my view of love. I asked him what he thought of it. His response was to tell me about a story that came to his mind as he listened to the Lemba narrative. Story awakens the memory of stories. In some cultures it is said they lean on each other. The context of the storytelling is vital to understanding the way in which stories function for every sort of teaching, sharing, and healing in the Mende tradition of his birth.

Context

Every evening in the village of Mattru Jong, young and old sat in a circle and exchanged stories, particularly during harvest season. Each person was expected to tell or retell a story as part of the evening event. A stone might be passed from one person to the next. Children were taught to listen carefully because they were also expected to repeat stories that they had heard. My son is and was an excellent listener. He has the capacity bred from his history of story-listening to reflect instantly on what he hears.

. . .

An older man told this tale:[21]

A young boy went into the bush to hunt with his bow and arrow. He saw a monkey on the branch of a tree and aimed his arrow. The monkey spoke to him: "Stop. You must think before you shoot me. If you kill me, your mother will die and if you do not kill me, your father will die."

Each person was then asked to discuss the story and what he or she thought the boy should do. Everyone had an opinion. Ishmael could not remember what each person had said because he was too busy trying to find his own answer at the time. He was afraid that if he made either choice, then either his mother or father would think he favored one of them. So he refused to give an answer and ran away. He said, "I ran away rather than have to make a choice." As he ran he had an answer that he records in his memoir, *A Long Way Gone*.

Needless to say, the story haunted me.

"What a strange story to tell, and to leave without an ending!" I thought.

I could not rest easily with this story. Obviously, having heard it so long ago and still remembering it so vividly, Ishmael could not forget it either. He had, in fact, been talking about hunting in the bush just days before. He told me about the most remarkable animal that did not have any paws. It had to pull itself everywhere, and when it wanted to run on the ground, it knocked a hard fruit onto the earth to scatter any enemies, human or animal, and then threw itself to the ground to make its escape. It poignantly reminded me of the children who lost arms and legs during the war he was caught in for years.

In the middle of the next night, I woke up and thought about the story. I thought that perhaps, since the actual story is not the words alone but how it lives in the listener, it also might be about the fact that death is inescapable. It was true that no matter who the boy chose, both his parents would ultimately die, as would the boy and the monkey.

Then I thought about the monkey who stopped the boy's mind from hunting at that moment to reflect on what he was doing. He was taking a life and all things taken are repaid in some way in the energy of the world.

He had also hesitated when about to hunt. Can a hunter afford to think about the outcome of his action when he is hunting? Does he not need to think only about what he is doing and the food he is taking?

Then I thought about the whole process of listening and thinking at a profound level, rather than always getting spoon-fed a simple answer for our stories. Here was a living example of the power of story to heal and keep the mind alive, since it put us face to face with the most challenging dilemmas: to not be afraid of the difficult questions and life-risking activities; to look at and think about death, about hunting of every sort, and about our process of making sense of stories. In the end, I am struck by the generosity of the storyteller, who allowed everyone to come up with answers, rather than having one right answer. Also, an amazing confidence in children was expressed, since it allowed them as well to live into this story for a long time.

At the depth of the story were important possible reflections. If we are patient we will make room for many answers, and accept that in some circumstances, there may be no answers.[22]

Give more of your life to this listening.

As brightness is to time, so you are to the one

who talks to the deep ear in your chest.

I should sell my tongue and buy a thousand ears

when that one steps near and begins to speak.

—RUMI

On Listening

I RECOGNIZE THE FULL importance and benefit of genuine deep listening. This listening is a discerning of what is actually happening in a narrative from what I assume, and the ability to hear what others are saying even in the silence of their being an audience. Such listening is the heart of how I might benefit as a storyteller. My continuous practice is to deepen access to this innate, often half-asleep, capacity. Standing in the way are assumptions, usually garnered from habit, interpretation, or beliefs, that color the intention of the spoken event. I have had to ripen my hearing with diligence to clarify and trust the intelligence of my ears so my stories can penetrate with the least manipulation. True listening is sublime protection. It is the engine of the reciprocity that for me signifies an enlivened and potent performance.

Some knowledge of how image and event can be fundamentally imagined and felt in the mind of the audience is as important as my awareness of what is happening in the story. It is a felt sense that takes careful investigation of the "facts" of the story as a whole. I cannot know what my audience actually hears and associates or imagines; however, I can spy at my own intentions and uncover the underground rivers of engendered journey that a story can provide. Although I think that listening is natural to us all, it demands great attention because it is easily forgotten. Most of us have not been trained to use our unbiased ears with confidence.

My training has arisen from experience as a teller of tales, and as many years in the practice of mindfulness-awareness meditation. I have found that listening demands a willingness to become alert to my own thoughts and opinions, while maintaining an open ear to distinguish between them and what is being said. The insight that arises from "resting the mind" in contemplative practice becomes useful when put to the test in everyday experience. Coming to "read" my own habitual, sometimes unconscious stories that can obstruct hearing, and feeling into my audience while seeing the storyline clearly, is a vital regimen of discipline and delight. The practice of meditation offers a very practical and direct way to experience the difference between being caught up in thoughts and the abiding sense of space from which these thoughts arise, natural to the totality of our minds. The traditional metaphor is of the difference between the vast blue sky and the clouds that often veil its constant presence.

In a book about Chinese art, I read that "First, you have to look in order to see, and you have to hear in order to listen." The text went on to explain that if you see without looking, you will see only what you already know: projecting your own sense of things and not allowing reality to be perceived as it is. The same thing happens if we half-listen without hearing. We won't hear what's actually being said, but will make a fast leap of understanding based on what we assume. Or, even more dangerous, a storyteller might decide for an audience how they should understand the meaning of the story—making it into propaganda, and no longer a living, breathing narrative whose meaning penetrates because it is an experience. I believe that fundamentalism is the belief that only one story is true, and that only one story *can* be true. It doesn't allow space for anyone else's stories. I remember hearing a Native American woman say, "The stories of my culture are best." But she quickly added, "We all say that, don't we?" Because she knew that, she could co-exist.

To give you a sense of what I mean, I'm going to relate a story from Northern Korea about listening, and weave it through this narrative. I hope it offers an experience of the journey of opening the unbiased ear even while it is read on a page.

....

There was a boy who longed to hear the sound of no sound. His village was surrounded by forests and mountains in a valley of waterfalls, and there was never a moment of silence. He became adept at hearing the varied sounds of the wind or the rippling echoes of water falling into water. He preferred to be alone so he could search for this unusual desire. His parents hoped that he would give it up and find pleasure in what other young men his age enjoyed, for spending so much time alone was considered unnatural in his culture.

One day he begged to leave. He promised his mother and father that if he could walk beyond the sound of water to hear true silence, he would spend less time alone on his return. Finally, they agreed.

The boy climbed into the mountains. He was able to travel safely beyond the last falls by recognizing the sounds of the water. As he walked on he finally arrived at a place where the sounds of wind and water ceased. He realized his wish. Happily, he traveled further and continued to listen, resting his ears in the absence of sound. But when he decided to return home, he was unable to find his way. He became lost because he had no memory of shape or inner map that was not defined by familiar sound.

I have always wondered how the boy in this tale knew that there could be an absence of sound. I imagine that his curiosity, alive through the discipline of hearing, awoke this question, just as each of us wonders from time to time, so caught in the momentum of our lives, what it might be like to die or be without our ever-present thoughts.

Many years ago, I recorded a weekly radio storytelling program for adults. Sometimes I invited storytellers visiting Manhattan from different parts of the world to share their stories or music.

Ephat Mujuru, a Shona singer and teller from Zimbabwe who sadly died a few years ago, was one such guest. He played his mbira (thumb piano) continuously throughout the interview. When I inquired why he sometimes began his stories at the start of a show while other times he played the mbira, sang, moved around the stage, and then began, he said he was educated by his grandparents, who were diviners. He explained that he was mostly taught to listen. "I learned that when you finally feel you are at the fifth stage of listening with your audience, they are ready to hear the story." I was about to ask what that was, when I became aware that the rhythm of the mbira kept changing, and I was overcome by the enchantment of the sound. "It is something I cannot explain," he added. I felt it, however, as he began a story about the importance of tradition.

On another program I asked teachers to come and speak about stories and listening in the classroom. A Montessori teacher spoke about how young children love to tell her fragments of stories. Then she related an experience. She had set up activities for all the children so they would work at different tables with different tasks. Everyone was completely engaged, except one little boy who seemed to be doing nothing. He was rocking back and forth on a rocking chair. She asked him, "Don't you want to do something?" He replied, "I am doing something!" "What do you think you are doing?" He answered, "I'm listening!"

Twenty years later, after a tiring day of my telling stories in schools in Seattle, Skagit elder Vi Hilbert caught me up in a long description of shamanic healing that took place in the long-house when she was a child. My mind began wandering. Although I was interested, I felt too tired to concentrate. "Excuse me," I said. "I am not focused." Like a canoe changing directions, she immediately began to tell me the story of a young orphan girl abandoned on an island who learned about cedar from the cedar trees themselves. Suddenly, I came awake. Vi ended the tale, asking me, "So. Do you think that the shamans knew magic?" A bit stunned by the question, I tried to recall what she had said earlier. I answered, "Yes. They must have been trained in magic." She said, "No. They knew how to listen."

A final example is my telling Alusine Bah the tale of "The Magic Finger" in a taxi on the way to JFK Airport, on the trip that would take him back to the war in Sierra Leone. As I described in "Sudden Story," he was sobbing because he feared the return. I entreated him to stop crying so he could return to Africa without throwing himself into a state of trauma, and when I asked him what I could do he asked for a story. Not knowing what to do I simply chose a story that rose up in the awkward unknowing of that moment. Personally, I think the time when I didn't know what to do, the time when I was at a loss for what to say, a moment without my concepts of how to help him, was the time of deep listening that brought forth the memory of a story. I wasn't logically deciding what story to tell. It was only once the story was told, and Alusine responded by saying that he understood that the boy in the story was asking for the personal inherent confidence to know his future, that I realized I had trusted my inner ear.

In "The Boy Who Loved Silence," the boy had to experience all aspects of listening not only to what he heard, but to the ceaseless lake of no sound out of which all sounds arise.

Exploring an exercise taught by drummer Jerry Granelli, I had high school students close their eyes, open their ears, and listen to the panoply of sounds in a room. After listing how many things they heard, I urged them to try and listen to the sounds in their own bodies. Finally, I asked them to listen even more deeply to see if they could hear the silence between sounds. A boy related, "I heard it. It was like the sound of snow in the distance before it falls." Once we had practiced this activity, opening the gates to expansive presence, our listening to stories and our listening to each other both transformed dramatically.

When I teach workshops and discuss listening with an audience, certain themes often come to the forefront. Some people talk about how they relax while the story unfolds. Some mention that they begin by listening analytically, even watching my technique and wondering what I'm doing to achieve each effect. But as the story progresses, they "get lost" in wanting to know what is going to happen next, until even that is not what is happening. They become the story, viscerally creating it in their own minds. If I asked for more details about their experience, they noted that they had been lost in the story, but were also aware that they were hearing a story in a room with others.

Will we lose our capacity to listen or seek out stories if we spend time endlessly projected into a digital world where images are pre-constructed for us, where voices are more and more unfeeling, saying one thing but meaning another? What happens when we grow accustomed as we have in the last hundred years to sales pitches and sound bites, mistaking them for oral tradition because they are spoken? Or when we cannot recognize when someone is acting an emotion or explaining an emotion, rather than their voices expressing a feeling that touches us beneath the realm of intellect. Perhaps most insidious is thinking that the story is the explanation of what we mean rather than manifesting it between ourselves and others so it can be known...undergone...lived. The deep listening engendered by living storytelling allows us to hear a true voice and respond directly without having to translate or interpret. It offers an invitation to be present, moment by moment, with intelligence and the vividness of waking dream.

Robert Bringhurst says "A story is not a house...it is an occurrence."

Will we be afraid of silence if we are not offered the opportunity to uncover our natural resources of listening? Can we hear silence? Is it devoid of sound? There is a Zen koan that asks:

What do you hear?

What do you hear?

In this reflection, what happens to us is more informative than an explanation. I think that recognizing the visceral benefits of listening to stories can provide a healing or an antidote to this kind of biased hearing based on selling rather than connecting.

> The knower of the mystery of sound knows the mystery of the whole universe.
>
> —Hazrat Inayat Khan

> The young man wandered lost for a long time without food or warm clothes in the increasing cold of the mountain forest, until he heard the sound of water trickling down stones. He rushed toward a clear pool where he saw a young woman in a blue silk dress standing by the water. The girl cast no reflection and he was terrified that she was a ghost. He fled without drinking, but could not live without water. Urged by thirst and the hope of finding his way home, he retraced his steps—but found no pool and no girl.

Stories trick us into natural synchronization of mind and body so that we can't help but listen. Our desire to know what is going to happen next is supported by the fact that we construct the only landscape on which the story occurs. Words spoken directly become our images, even if the images are self-created and not the same as anyone else's. We become concerned with the destiny of the characters because they arise out of our own minds. To see them is not the hook; rather the ear of our engaged eye pulls us more deeply into the story. There's nothing devious or manipulative about it if the storyteller is dedicated to sharing the story rather than their personal version or explanation. Visual visceral listening is the natural response to spoken story. We are urged by a thirst for what is going to happen next. Our lives sometimes seem to depend on it.

The next day, he heard the sound of water again, and followed it until he saw the same girl standing by a stream. This time, he bent down to drink. At that moment the girl disappeared and in her place hovered a small blue bird. The young man followed her as if pulled forward in a dream.

> Whether we believe in ghosts or not, we have all had moments where the possibility of something "other" has startled us and allowed us to suspect there is more than what we identify as real. Perhaps it was a sound in the night on a dark road, or a weirdly shaped shadow adorning the sound of an uncanny wind. Our ears satisfy their thirst for more.

The bird led him up to a cave deep in the rocks. There sat an old Buddhist monk in yellow robes. The old man held a wooden staff in one hand and in the other a fan made of crane feathers. He offered the boy food and water. The bird vanished.

The man said, "I was waiting for you."

The boy answered, "I have been looking for you as long as I can remember."

The monk was the guardian of the mountain and the caretaker of the people in the villages below. "I am very old. It is your turn to learn the teachings of kindness and wisdom and take my place."

From that day onwards, the boy became a student. He remained in the cave and studied, learned to meditate and pray. The boy who knew the sound of water and silence learned to listen with greater care.

In the mountains, the old monk died. In the village, meanwhile, everyone mourned the death of the boy, whom they were sure had met ill fortune on his journey in the mountains.

As the years passed, pilgrims in need of help, or travelers happening upon the cave, received kindness or healing from the monk who had taken the old man's place. He taught them prayers, told them tales, or often sat in a silence that brought peace to their worried minds.

When we hear a story I suspect that this engagement is so familiar and refreshing that we hang on the words not only to enjoy the outcome of the tale, but to remain in contact with the unbiased ear that has opened in our heart at the same time.

Words spoken are only a part of conversation and storytelling. When I am telling a story, I experience a sort of double or triple listening. It's not at all self-conscious or intellectual (as it would be, for example, if I was trying to remember the words of the story or make sure my listener aligns with my favorite meaning or character). It feels natural. I am listening to my listeners all the time. It is as if we were meeting both in our room and in a mountain cave unseen. The unfolding of the story, the timing, doesn't come so much from me as from this relationship. In the best of times, we are present together, breathing, imagining, and deep in active listening, and still aware of being in the room together. It's almost as if I think of something, they visualize it, and then I describe it.

This quality of reciprocity is tingly with life. If I attempt to grasp at it intellectually I lose the connection. Self-consciousness would get in the way and I might find myself estranged on a solo trip. When minds and bodies are synchronized in this way, we can access a vast and wakeful space that lies beneath our thinking mind.

I used to do workshops for teachers after their classes ended for the day. I would walk in and encounter people who looked wilted and seemed stressed out. Instead of launching into my "lessons" or "how to's" I would spend twenty minutes telling stories. As they listened, these 'wilted' people would perk up, as if I'd poured water on their roots. But if I entered the same situation without paying attention to their depleted state and began demanding their attention to my information, they dutifully took notes but remained passive, or even irritated. The telling was my means of gathering them back into their capacity to be present by accessing their own innate ocean of stillness, always available.

One summer, the monk thought of the sound of the waterfalls. He knew he had to return to his village. He walked down the scraggy pathways and finally arrived at the top of the highest falls. His ears quickly remembered the sounds like a language never forgotten. He felt no joy or relief, however. He heard something ominous in the gurgle of the water—a warning of impending danger.

Rushing as fast as he could he ran to his village and found his mother and father. He told them who he was and what he had heard in the water. News passed from house to house and most people began to leave with only what they could carry. They climbed higher and higher into the mountains. Behind them the water rose, fierce and furious, flooding the valley that they had known as home.

All those who heeded the warning survived and made a new village close to the cave where the monk lived. Without the ears that had learned to read the sound of the world, all the villagers would have been destroyed.

....

The listening aspect of storytelling is what renders the experience beneficial and also penetrating. What is uncovered within us and practiced is the ability to discern what we are assuming and what we are hearing. Our capacity to open into a more expansive sense of abiding presence is strengthened so that we can not only "cope" but find joy and relief in all that we do. The process, like the journey of a story, takes time, patience, and longing. I encourage us to explore what is this space of open, unbiased listening that can be found within us all, and which empowers and nourishes.

The first step is to know it exists and that is an experience. The next is to become aware of our own bestoried minds that obstruct us from what is actually happening in the room, in our lives, or in the tales we are studying. Then, the practice and the learning about the depth of listening can be known, and then, naturally, the storytelling becomes an act of compassion because it is an offering that gently pries open the gates of joy and perception, in any circumstance. The alchemy is in the shared word that becomes everything possible or impossible.

When I invite people at the end to look around the room and see if the storytelling has made any difference to the quality of the space, they often say it feels smaller, less separate, warmer. More of a soft space to be. Sharing "the space of the story telling" when it is taking place is like hearing an affectionate whisper that is deeply nourishing. We know we can trust ourselves and our world beyond our usual pre-packaged projections, habitual repetitions and distractions, because we actually experience the source of our intelligence in action, communally, re-creating the story.[23]

O listen—

Listen more carefully

To what is inside of you right now.

In my world

All that remains is the wondrous call to

Dance and Prayer

Rising up like a thousand suns

Out of the mouth of a

Single Bird.

—Hafiz

Afterword

THE TALE OF "THE Hen and the Rooster" is a route that takes us home, where we seek with our hero what was lacking that would render a kingdom whole. What took place was not what was expected. However, the youngest prince, and hence we listeners, have traveled where we normally would not have gone. Just as on my own journey, I have discovered so much that I would not have expected was called for in becoming a storyteller.

Vi Hilbert once told me that it was not my work to help her with the language and stories of her Skagit tribe that she had devoted her life to preserving. It was my job, she insisted, "to keep the spirit of story alive." I inquired what that was. She walked outside onto her porch that grey winter day, facing the sacred mountains of her people. She held up her right hand and began to sing in Lushootseed. The sky filled with birds and a crow alighted on her palm. The crow remained until her singing stopped. Then it flew away, as did all the other birds, including robins, ravens, and white trumpeter swans. Without discussion about what had occurred she went inside for a fresh cup of coffee, and I followed. Coming to the end of this book that explores more deeply what intrigued me about the fairytale, that event is illumined.

If I truly want to understand a story's significance, I look to the end of the tale. I look at the fruition or resolution. From back to start I note what had to happen for the outcome to be of benefit: for a union of opposites to occur, for a hero or heroine to become true rulers of their world, for wisdom and compassion to manifest fully, for whatever was lost to be found, or whatever was out of balance to be aligned. Seemingly repetitive events, confrontations, journeys to other realms, and obstacles overcome make sense in a new way. It is how I feel confident to hold my listeners through illogical or strange details. The events that are requisite for the alchemy of the inner lived story also model the patience we need to traverse uncomfortable or unfamiliar territory within ourselves to make meaning of our lives.

The story told is not for those in the tale, but for those hearing the tale. I pondered why the locked cage was seen for the first time at a late point in the narrative. I respect sudden appearances of image, character, or symbol just as I pay attention to the arrival of an image in an unforgettable dream.

Before the story could end and the prince could return to become the king, with the maiden as beloved, he had to release the captive water in the world below that had caused a drought, and save the eagle mother's babies from an insidious enemy rooted even deeper than the stone well and the dragon that parsed out the water and demanded the sacrifice of young women. Carried by the mother eagle, she who could soar between worlds, the youngest prince rediscovered the maiden waiting at the very place where the bald-headed lute player had carried her underground. It was the same place where our hero had untied ropes that bound him and gone in search of her not knowing how or where he would find her. He disobeyed the command of two magical servants, the transformed stirrups of two three-legged horses who had tied his legs to that place. If he had not disobeyed he would never have made the full journey. He leapt onto the back of another three-legged horse in a craggy field and was carried downwards to the achingly dry world. Remoisturizing the place below, he was able to ascend again. Isn't that what we must so often do in our lives to truly transform our circumstances? Don't we need to make moist what has grown stale?

I trust that the sequence of events present themselves when my listeners' thirst is quenched enough that they can surrender to what happens next. Perhaps this process of events renders us ready to intuit why the hen and rooster were needed for the completion of a holy edifice and the coronation of a genuine king and queen, within ourselves and in our world. To wake up is not easy. The path is never what we expect. The story imagined, felt, and created within is a template or a practice for our own liberation.

The maiden with long hair was already there on a cloud in the other world at the start of the tale. Only the storyteller knew that. The hero went in search of the male and female birds. Only the storyteller knew that without the maiden they could not be taken. She was dangerous in the daylight, but could be coerced in the darkness of night. Only the old man who was watering corn with a bucket full of holes knew the way. And that way was ultimate kindness. "Noble horse. I need you." As the story came to an end, we came to know that her liberation depended not only on the perseverance and kindness of the hero, but on all the events and the liberation of the bald-headed lute player, who was assumed to be evil or an obstacle to the prince's success.

The lute-player's image delighted me, although I had no idea who he was or what he was doing asleep on the cloud beneath her when I first told the story. Slowly moving backwards, I recognized that he was not playing his music while his heart, strength, and life force were imprisoned in the cage with nine locks. He wanted the maiden and the birds, it seemed, yet when he caught her he carried her down beneath that world and then flew back to the cloud and returned to sleep. When the hero rediscovered the maiden he said, "How can I destroy the bald-headed lute player?" So often we want to destroy what seems to be our ill fortune, but again we are surprised. It was not necessary to destroy him, she explained. It was necessary to open the nine locks and let the three birds free so he could play his music. What mysterious alchemy is at work here? It moves me as deeply as Vi's words and the reality of the crow on her palm. I find myself grateful to the lute player for forcing the hero to go where he would never have traveled so the source of the blockage in our tale could be opened.

The perfect outer form may be achieved, but without an enlivened heart, informed by love and compassion, the temple remains empty. There is no fresh rulership possible. Without compassion, the words of a storyteller as well remain just words. It is not until I studied the story in reverse that I recognized why it was fit to weave throughout this book, and how personal it was to me and I hope to others.

Was the whole story meant for the ultimate completion of a sacred place so there would be genuine rulership? Was the adventure carried out so the stones of the well and the greed of the dragon could be removed? Was the dilemma resolved by the wedding of the risk-taking prince and the maiden with the hen and rooster? Or was it to release music into the world? Or to transform aggression caused by lack of heart, spirit, and inner strength? Or something more?

I am reminded of the teachings of the Sakyong Mipham Rinpoche, who called happiness "turning the flower outwards." Compassion for others brings joy, and thinking of only ourselves brings unhappiness, he stated. The embodied journey of the story within us is a mirror that shows us that turning the flower outwards happens when we are inspired to turn the mirror inwards. The conclusion brings new life into the world. The hen and the rooster produce an egg. The spirit of story is our protection. It can short-circuit our habitual tales, those we tell ourselves that are drought-producing, as dangerous as the dragon. And in the telling again and again, for the benefit of ourselves and others, we render whole and find ourselves present to the vast story that is always there, which has no words.

Notes

1. Peter Brook, *The Open Door* (New York: Pantheon, 1993).

2. Helene Cixous, *Three Steps on the Ladder to Writing* (New York: Columbia University Press, 1993).

3. Jane Harrison, *Ancient Art and Ritual*, (Bradford- on-Avon, England: Moonraker Press, 1978).

4. Michael Wood, *The Smile of Murrigan* (London: Penguin, 1996).

5. Lucy Menzies, *Caucasian Folktales* (London: J.M. Dent & Sons, 1925).

6. The Bushman story is retold from a tale recorded by Sir Laurens Van Der Post.

7. *The Philippine Handbook.*

8. Florence Alterman is my father's sister. This was part of a family history tape I recorded in the fall of 1982.

9. Helen M. Luke, *The Inner Story* (New York: Crossroad, 1982). This is transcribed from my retelling of the story for performance.

10. Joseph Campbell, *Myths to Live By* (New York: Bantam, 1973), chapter 1. Fritjof Capra, *The Tao of Physics* (Berkeley: Shambhala, 1975). Ruth Finnegan, *Oral Poetry: Its History, Significance and Social Function* (Cambridge: Cambridge University Press, 1977). Colin M. Turnbull, *The Human Cycle* (New York: Simon & Schuster, 1983).

11. Laurens van der Post, *Patterns of Renewal* (Wallingford, PA: Pendle Hill Publications, 1979), p.11.

12. Richard Leakey and Roger Lewin, *People of the Lake* (New York: Anchor Press, 1978), p. 194-221.

13. See Laura Simms, "Storytelling, Children and Imagination," *Texas Library Journal*, Winter 1981, for discussion of the form of the ritual process between storyteller and listener.

14. See Laura Simms, "Words in our Hearts," *Hornbook Magazine*, June 1983, for discussion on relationship between listeners and storytellers.

15. "...it has probably never been more necessary to proclaim, as do the myths, that sound humanism does not begin with oneself, but puts the world before life, life before man, and respect for others before self-interest..." Claude Levi-Strauss, *The Origin of Table Manners: Introduction to a Science of Mythology, Vol. III* (New York: Harper and Row, 1978), p. 508.

16. Malidoma Patrice Somé, *Ritual* (New York: Penguin, 1997), p. 3.

17. Special thanks to Jean Sviadac and Walter Feldman for their help with writing this chapter.

18. Jalaloddin Rumi, Coleman Barks, trans., *The Glance* (New York: Putman Books, 1999).

19. This tale was told to me by Pomme Clayton in London. I retell it with her permission.

20. Ishmael has written his own memoir that has become a bestselling book, *A Long Way Gone* (New York: Farrar, Straus and Giroux, 2008).

21. At the very end of my son's memoir, *A Long Way Gone*, he also reflects on this story that he remembered that evening and also recalls having reheard in Washington, D.C.

22. Written for the Treasure House page on healingstory.org in 2004.

23. This chapter is based on a talk that I gave in Salt Lake City to a class of teachers at the University of Utah, taught by Leslie Kelen, 2006. I recommend reading the chapter "Temple in the Ear" in the book *Nada Brahma: The World Is Sound*, by Joachim-Ernst Berendt (Rochester, VT: Destiny Books, 1987) for a deeper discussion of the difference between voiding sound and listening to silence.

Acknowledgments

My work would not have been possible without the pointing out instructions of the Vidhyadhara Chogyam Trungpa, Rinpoche; Venerable Dzigar Kongtrul, Rinpoche; The Sakyong Mipham, Rinpoche; and the unsurpassable inspiration of my sister on the path Terry Tempest Williams. From Terry I learn to always go deeper with fierce open heart. Throughout my career I have had the great fortune to be a student of living "scholars" of story. Especially, revered Salish elder Vi Taqseblu Hilbert—you were like a mother; Monsieur Jean Sviadoc, who offered me one wisdom tale after another; and my beloved friends Muriel Bloch, Dan Yashinsky, Connie Regan Blake, Gioia Timpanelli and Barbara Koltuv—beacons of light. And my teacher Joseph Campbell, who told me that "all of life is a story."

There are those whose insight and inspiration have changed my life, whom I have not met, but who have been companions: Robert Bringhurst, Ted Chamberlain, Amadou Hampate Ba, Marcel Griaule, Helene Cixous, and Linda Hogan. Your words sustain. There are innumerable teachers and friends. I have a special thank you to Jerry Wennstrom for fearless authenticity and love of story, and to Paula Allen, who galloped into my life and roams the meadow of activism and motherhood with full force. I offer special thanks to poet/philosopher David Appelbaum. Without my close friends many hard times would not have been transformed. Deep gratitude for shared stories: Valerie Lorig, Shelley Pierce, Mishko Manuel, Merrinell Phillips, Mark

Horn, Heather Forest, Milbre Burch, Joseph Sobel, Richard Reoch, Emily Nash, Steve Gorn, Angela Lloyd, Cathy Chilco, Aldo Civico, Julia Haines, Deena Metzger, Diane Nadler, Barbara Borden, Naomi Newman, and Walter Feldman. To Jack Zimmerman, a special bow for council and true listening. I also want to thank the myriad young people throughout the world whose wide eyed listening is my motivation. Daily I think of the youth I met in Northern Romania, Nepal, Philippines, and Haiti.

And, gratitude to Ishmael, my son, for telling his story and giving me the knowledge of being a mother; to Alusine for never forgetting what is good; to my brother who read me Chaucer and Shakespeare; and my mother and father.

Much of the material in this book was formerly published in the following places, and appears here in edited versions.

"Crossing into the Invisible," appeared in *Parabola Magazine*, Spring 2000.

"What Storytelling Means to Me," appeared in *Tale Trader Newspaper*, August 1995.

"Summoning the Realm of Dream," appeared in *Storytelling Magazine*, September 1996.

"Seeing the Invisible," appeared in *Humanity Magazine*, July 1996.

"The Secret Practice," appeared in *Parabola Magazine*, Summer 1995.

"T'Boli Dreaming," appeared in *Organica Magazine*, Spring/Summer 1996.

"The Lamplighter: the Storyteller in the Modern World," appeared in *National Storytelling Journal*, Winter 1984.

"Evil in the World," appeared on HasidicStories.com, © Laura Simms, 1997.

"Another Way of Knowing," appeared in *Organica Magazine*, Winter 1996.

"Misfortune's Fortune," appeared in *Parabola Magazine*, Winter 2000.

"A Language of No Words," appeared in *Tell the World: Storytelling Across Language Barriers*, 2007.

"Natural Interruptions," appeared in *Parabola Magazine*, Spring 1999.

"Journey to Jerusalem," appeared in *Shambhala Sun*, July 1995.

"Sudden Story," appeared in *The Storytelling Magazine*, January/February 1995.

"Deadly Play," appeared in *Shambhala Sun*, January 1999.

"Strong Medicine," appeared in *Diving in the Moon Magazine*, Summer 2008.

"Monkey Mind" appeared on HealingStory.org, © Laura Simms, Fall 2000.

About the Author

Laura Simms is an award-winning storyteller, recording artist, teacher, writer, and humanitarian based in New York City. *The New York Times* has called her "a major force in the revival of storytelling in America." Remarkable performances of traditional stories interwoven with personal narrative have earned her worldwide recognition and honors since 1968. Laura has created an irresistible cutting-edge performance style that bridges ancient oral tradition and performance art. Her storytelling is meaningful and uncannily entertaining for her international audiences. Her warmth, depth of understanding, profound effect on listeners, diverse material, humor, gorgeous voice, and range of characterizations are her trademarks.

Her most recent one-woman show, *Mercy into the World*, premiered in 2008 at the Barbican Theater in London, University of Oslo, and Frontier Theater in Winnipeg, Manitoba. She has performed at venues worldwide, including the Khan Theater in Jerusalem, Royal Festival Hall in London, The Central Theater of Manila, and Victory Theater and Town Hall in New York City.

Laura works with international organizations to train teachers and humanitarian workers. She received the Brimstone Award for Engaged Storytelling and is co-faculty with Terry Tempest Williams for the New Generation Environmental Project. She is the mother of Ishmael Beah, bestselling author of *A Long Way Gone*. Under a grant from Mercy Corps, Laura twice took her storytelling work to New Orleans for teachers and children in post-Katrina New Orleans. Most recently she began a storytelling project with International Medical Corps in Haiti. Her website is www.laurasimms.com.

Sentient Publications, LLC publishes books on cultural creativity, experimental education, transformative spirituality, holistic health, new science, ecology, and other topics, approached from an integral viewpoint. Our authors are intensely interested in exploring the nature of life from fresh perspectives, addressing life's great questions, and fostering the full expression of the human potential. Sentient Publications' books arise from the spirit of inquiry and the richness of the inherent dialogue between writer and reader.

Our Culture Tools series is designed to give social catalyzers and cultural entrepreneurs the essential information, technology, and inspiration to forge a sustainable, creative, and compassionate world.

We are very interested in hearing from our readers. To direct suggestions or comments to us, or to be added to our mailing list, please contact:

SENTIENT PUBLICATIONS, LLC
1113 Spruce Street
Boulder, CO 80302
303-443-2188
contact@sentientpublications.com
www.sentientpublications.com